Women of Virtue
Walking in Excellence

Inspirational Stories of Character, Wisdom, Courage and Strength

VISIONARY AUTHOR
DR. TASHEKA L. GREEN

For information regarding special discounts for bulk purchases, please contact the publisher: LaBoo Publishing Enterprise, LLC

staff@laboopublishing.com
www.laboopublishing.com

Table of Contents

Foreword

Women of Virtue Walking in Excellence: Inspirational Stories of Character, Wisdom, Courage, and Strength is a compilation of short narratives from twenty virtuous women who were inspired to share their stories. Visionary author Dr. Tasheka L. Green executed the vision that God gave her to bring together women of all ethnic groups, backgrounds, and nationalities to share their stories, which focus on the walk they had to embark on to get to where they are today. So often, people see the product, but they do not see the process one has to go through. In this best-selling self-help book, these women embrace their walk and overcome with their testimony, great power, grace, and worth. These women not only walked in excellence, but they demonstrated excellence through their character, wisdom, courage, and strength. *Women of Virtue Walking in Excellence: Inspirational Stories of Character, Wisdom, Courage, and Strength* is an easy-to-read page-turner that will inspire you to be the best version of you. These authentic and compelling stories will capture your heart, transform your mind, and motivate you to pursue all that God has for you.

As a Woman of Virtue Walking in Excellence, my passion is toward helping others to become financially literate, stable, and prepared for the future. I have been dedicated to the call to help others by leading and facilitating various financial literacy outreach programs and platforms. I have had the opportunity to travel world-wide to champion this call. However, my heart has a special place just for women. My 'yes' to this call did not come without a price. The 'yes' to this call cost some loss, hurt, pain, failure, disappointments, family members, friends, and/or tangible things. It did not bring me to a lowly place, but it brought me to a humbling place that prepared me for a greater place, to help and impact more people.

Years ago, my husband passed away, leaving me with a lot of responsibility and three children to take care of, including a one-year-old. Within a moment, I had become a single mother without the means to take care of my family. During this time, I had to balance my emotions between the loss of my husband and being strong for my family, and to try to make ends meet with what I had left. It was especially difficult because not only was I alone, but I did not have any financial support. This made the process even more challenging, leaving me with uncertainty as to how I would survive. I had to stand in my character, walk in wisdom, become courageous, and use the strength I did not know I even had to ensure that not only would my family and I survive, but we would thrive. I had to walk in the ways of a virtuous woman because my family not only needed me, but they were counting on me. I could not go looking for the answer; I had to become the answer. In this very moment, I knew that this was not the end of my story. So I began to rewrite my story so that other women would not find themselves in the space in which I was, feeling helpless, hopeless, and alone. At this moment, I had to be the example for other women to see that we as women need to be more proactive and aware when it comes to being financially literate, whether if it is for yourself or the affairs of family members.

Dr. Tasheka L. Green has the same belief and passion for helping others by making life and situations better for everyone. Her heart toward inspiring and serving others is the foundation for the conception of this book. The message that resounds in this book captures the essence that as a woman of virtue walking in excellence, you should not only be surviving, but you should be thriving in every area of your life. If you are not, the only one holding you back is you. Just as I too had to step up to the call, you to have to step up to the call of being the women of virtue you were designed to be. There are so many people who are waiting for you to be the answer that they need. You were created to be an answer, successful, great and influential to everyone you teach, reach, or meet.

Women of Virtue Walking in Excellence, be so great that you cannot be ignored or overlooked. Stand confidently in your character, wisdom, courage, and strength, so that you do not have to go looking for anything or anyone; they will come looking for you, because you are the answer that they need. Therefore, "Who can find a virtuous woman? For her price is far above rubies." Your answer to this question should be, "I am her. I am a woman of virtue." So I encourage you to walk in the ways of a virtuous woman and demonstrate excellence along the way. There is so much greatness on the inside of you. Pursue the journey with a purpose to discover how great you can be because you are a "Woman of Virtue Walking in Excellence: Character, Wisdom, Courage, and Strength."

Dr. Shirley Luu
Founder & CEO
Shirley Luu & Associates
Financial Services & Insurance
ShirleyLuuAssociates.com

Introduction

Being a Woman of Virtue Walking in Excellence is not about being perfect, but rather it is about living a purposeful life, and daily demonstrating this through character, wisdom, courage, and strength.

Women of Virtue Walking in Excellence: Inspirational Stories of Character, Wisdom, Courage, and Strength is a compilation of 21 diverse stories of women who demonstrate excellence in different areas of their lives, as told by wives, mothers, grandmothers, leaders, entrepreneurs, career women, inspirational speakers, ministers, transformational coaches, mentors, volunteers, and educators. We are not perfect, but we were created by a perfect God and seek to live a purposeful life with power, grace, and value.

These stories will transform your life, leaving you inspired to walk in the ways of a virtuous woman, to demonstrate excellence through character, wisdom, courage, and strength. The contributing authors in this book share their journeys, lessons, and the aspects that contributed to them being women of virtue who walk in excellence. Five years ago, when God gave me the vision of Women of Virtue Walking in Excellence, it was used as a platform to celebrate my mother's life, honor her greatness, and continue her legacy. My mother passed away in 2010 at the tender age of 53. She was diagnosed in February of 2010 with stage 4 stomach cancer, and passed away 30 days later, on March 30, 2010. I could have chosen to mourn and stay in an isolated, depressed state, or I could turn the mourning into dancing, the weeping into joy, and the isolation into celebration. Rather than mourning, weeping, and being isolated, I chose the latter: dancing, joy, and celebration.

With that being said, Women of Virtue Walking in Excellence evolved into The Deborah C. Offer Bulgin Women of Virtue Walking in Excellence Award. This award is given in memory of my mother, who truly was a woman of virtue who walked in excellence. The award is provided to virtuous women who have contributed to the improvement of and made an influential impact in the lives of others. Their leadership and dedication in changing the way of life for others, has proven why they are well deserving of this award. Not only did Women of Virtue Walking in Excellence result in celebrating other virtuous women, but it birthed The Deborah C. Offer Bulgin Memorial Scholarship, Daughters of Virtuous Women, Women of Virtue Walking in Excellence Conference, and this book, *Women of Virtue Walking in Excellence: Inspirational Stories of Character, Wisdom, Courage, and Strength.*

I have come to the realization that the choice to carry the mantle of my mother, live out the legacy she has prepared, and to pursue purpose, was bigger than my finite mind. If I had chosen to mourn, weep, and stay isolated, then I would have canceled all of the great things God has done, is doing, and will continue to do. Women of Virtue Walking in Excellence is exceedingly and abundantly above all I could ask or think. I have made a commitment to not do this alone, but to bring other women on this journey with me: married, single, divorced, mothers, grandmothers, sisters, volunteers, mentors, coaches, speakers, leaders, entrepreneurs, women who have been through a process and overcame; women who have a testimony, women who have a story, women who have love in their heart, women who are becoming, women who are virtuous, and women who are open, willing, and want to change themselves and lives across the world.

Thank you to all of the women who contributed to bringing this book into reality. Thank you for your openness, willingness, and compassion to be who God called you to be and fulfill His plan for your life. The women who committed to this work did not view it as an opportunity, but an assignment to inspire others through their stories, so after it is read, others would say, "Because of you I didn't give up."

DEFINING VIRTUE AND A VIRTUOUS WOMAN

As you embark upon reading the pages of this book, we must first define virtue and a virtuous woman. The word virtue means many different things but can be a trait or disposition of a person's character that is exemplified through their words and deeds. Someone with virtue displays wisdom, nobility, courage, kindness, good manners, courtesy, modesty, generosity, and self-control in their life. Virtuous people treat others fairly and esteem others highly. They love their neighbor as they love themselves (Matthew 22:39). Someone who has virtue has good, moral ethics and makes Godly choices in life.

"Who can find a virtuous woman? for her price is far above rubies" (Proverbs 31:10, KJV).

Did you know that rubies are one of the most popular gems derived from the mineral corundum? Corundum is the second-hardest natural mineral after a diamond. Corundum is one of the most highly desired jewelry stones. Rubies are one of the most valuable and popular of all corundum gemstones.

So now think about it..."Who can find a virtuous woman? for her price is far above rubies." Just to think that a virtuous woman's worth is far above rubies! Your worth cannot even be measured in earthly things, such as a rare stone like a ruby. Do you see how precious and valuable you are to God? Then every day, walk in that worth and demonstrate excellence through your words, actions, and deeds.

Women of Virtue Walking in Excellence know their worth, are not defined by their situation, and don't let others define them. When you know who you are and who you belong to; you know your worth. You have an inner beauty that only comes from God. You are fearfully and wonderfully made; marvelous are your works (Psalm 139:14). You use your creativity and uniqueness to create beauty in your life and the lives of others.

Have you ever wondered why the question in Proverbs 31:10 was proposed by Bathsheba to her son, King Lemuel, also known as Solomon, "Who can find a virtuous woman? for her price is far above rubies." With all of Solomon's wisdom, he says in Proverbs 18:22 (NKJV), "He who finds a wife finds a good thing and obtains favor from the Lord." Be mindful the words 'virtuous woman,' as mentioned above, are interchangeable with the word 'wife.'

Is it that virtuous women are hard to find? Is it that virtuous women are so esteemed and blessed by God that everything attached to them is also blessed? Then if this holds true, why are you not maximizing who you are and walking in the fullness of why you were uniquely created by God? You are an original masterpiece, sketched out, and patterned in the image of God. You are priceless, invaluable, worth it. There are qualities in you that were chosen just for you.

Just think, even when jewelers look at a gemstone, they look for the qualities of the gemstone. They look for the 4 Cs: Color, Clarity, Cut, and Carat.

Color: The way an object reflects light.

Clarity: Quality of being clear, transparency.

Cut: Not referring to shape, but the symmetry, proportioning and polish of a gemstone. The cut greatly affects the brilliance of the gemstone.

Carat: Unit of measurement.

So think about...What is your color? Are you reflecting light? Is your light shining brightly? You are full of purpose and promise. You do not have to chase people or opportunities; your light will have people and opportunities looking for you. Reflect the light!

How clear are you? You stand strong in your confidence and be certain of who you are, who you belong to, and what you have to offer. You set the standard! Don't let the standard set you!

Are you cut right? Are you proportional, well-balanced, skillful, and refined? If so, then you should be leveraging your skills, talents, and gifts to accomplish the intended plans of God for your life. Be a cut above the rest! You will never be unnoticed.

How are you measuring up? You are not an imitation or impostor. No comparison, no competition—there is only one you. Measure yourself up to your standards and expectations. Dr. Maya Angelou said, "Success is liking yourself, liking what you do, and liking how you do it."

As you continue to walk in excellence, worthy of what God called you to do, know your worth, know your value, own who you are, and become the best version of you.

The word virtuous occurs in the Bible on four occasions, in Proverbs 12:4, Proverbs 31:10, 31:29 and Ruth 3:11. In each case the word virtuous signifies character, wisdom, courage, and strength.

(Proverbs 12:4, KJV)

A virtuous woman is a crown to her husband: but she that maketh ashamed is as rottenness in his bones.

(Proverbs 31:10, KJV)

Who can find a virtuous woman? for her price is far above rubies.

(Proverbs 31:29, KJV)

Many daughters have done virtuously, but thou excellest them all.

(Ruth 3:11, KJV)

And now, my daughter, fear not; I will do to thee all that thou requirest: for all the city of my people doth know that thou art a virtuous woman.

When I researched the scriptures, there was only one woman in the Bible that was specifically called virtuous and her name was Ruth. According to Ruth 3:11, KJV, "And now, my daughter, fear not; I will do to thee all that thou requirest: for all the city of my people doth know that thou art a virtuous woman."

We can learn a lot from Ruth as we focus on women of virtue walking in excellence. It was through the eyes of Boaz that he acknowledged Ruth as a virtuous woman. There must have been something that was seen through her character, wisdom, courage, and strength that made her virtuous in the eyes of Boaz. Although I am referencing Ruth, many of the inspirational stories in this anthology exemplify several of the lessons that Ruth exhibited. Some of the lessons are as follows:

- Push Past Your Past and Pain
- Have Faith and Trust God
- Character Matters on the Journey to Promise
- Leave a Legacy Lineage

PUSH PAST YOUR PAST AND THE PAIN

Push past your past and pain by forgetting those things behind you and pressing toward what is ahead of you. The pain may be trouble, effort, and care to accomplish something, hurt, failures, regrets and/or fears. The first step to push past your past and pain is to renew your mind and forgive yourself. Once you forgive yourself, then begin the process of forgiving others. When you push past your past and the pain, you give yourself the permission and authorization to have the last word over your life. Your words should echo the voice of God and your life should reflect

His wonderful works. Do not let you past hold you back. "You may have done what they said you did, but you are not who they say you are" (Bishop Donald A. Wright, Senior Pastor, The Gathering at Forestville). Your name has significance, you have purpose, you were born to save lives and make a difference. Ruth didn't allow her past to hold her back, but believed there was life still to be lived and moved forward in character, wisdom, courage, and strength.

You have a purpose regardless of what lies behind you. Although your faith may waver, your purpose does not.

HAVE FAITH AND TRUST GOD

"Now faith is the substance of things hoped for, the evidence of things not seen" (Hebrews 11:1, KJV). "Without faith it is impossible to please Him" (Hebrews 11:6, KJV). "Faith without works is dead. Faith is trusting in the Lord with all your heart" (James 2:26, KJV). "Lean not to your own understanding. In all thy ways acknowledge Him and He shall direct thy path" (Proverbs 3:5-6, KJV). Ruth showed remarkable faith: faith that there was still a purpose for her ahead, faith to believe that God was who He said He was, and faith to believe that God would provide for her and Naomi. You might not be able to see what God is doing, nor do you understand it. You do not need to see or understand; you just need to trust that God is working everything out for your good. "And we know that all things work together for good to them that love God, to them who are the called according to His purpose" (Romans 8:28, KJV). Faith will build your character and give you courage to trust and believe. God will give you strength for the wait and grace for the process. Through this you will obtain wisdom to walk in the fullness of knowing that with God all things are possible.

CHARACTER MATTERS ON THE JOURNEY TO PROMISE

Character is who you are when nobody's watching. Ruth proved to be a woman of integrity with Boaz, so much so that he spoke over her and said, "And now, my daughter, fear not; I will do to thee all that thou requirest: for all the city of my people doth know that thou art a virtuous woman" (Ruth 3:11, KJV). Everything Ruth did represented a woman of great character, and God honored her. Ruth was friendly, determined, dedicated, obedient, humble—she was a virtuous woman. Be a woman of character, wisdom, courage, and strength. You do not have to recreate you, just be the woman God created you to be. Even though Ruth had lost her husband, she knew that there was a promise waiting for her. She was committed to her promise and submitted herself to Naomi. She never once stepped out of character. She remained authentic to who she was and was led by her heart and not her head. She knew that Naomi had what she needed to get her to where she needed to be.

"Watch your thoughts, for they become words. Watch your words, for they become actions. Watch your actions, for they become habits. Watch your habits, for they become character. Watch your character, for it will become your destiny." --Frank Outlaw

LEAVE A LEGACY LINEAGE

Legacy is not what you have accomplished, but it is rather what you have prepared others to do. "A good man leaveth an inheritance for his children's children" (Proverbs 13:22, KJV). One of the best parts of Ruth's story is the legacy God established through her. God brought her and Boaz together and they conceived a child. That child would be in the lineage of Jesus, the Savior of the world. Ruth's commitment to God and her purpose shows us that there is no limit to what God can do though us, in us and for us. The journey is not the destination, but the journey will take you to the destination, which becomes your destiny. Legacy is not quantifiable, but it is qualifiable by how you serve, love, give, help, support, and believe. Leave a legacy to your family that will allow others to see beyond temporal things to eternal things that can be passed on to ensure character, wisdom, courage and strength in others.

The story of Ruth shows how when you walk in the ways of a virtuous woman, you do not have to announce who you are; your words, actions, and deeds will speak for you, and others will know who you are and what you represent. The humility in your walk, the grace in your steps, and the authentic love in your heart will speak the profoundness of your character, wisdom, courage and strength. The inspirational stories in this anthology portray women whose words, actions, and deeds, were built on character, wisdom, courage, and strength. They could have given up, thrown in the towel, and walked away, but they refused to give up because they knew if they did, they would be giving up on God and purpose. Purpose focuses you when people and noises try to distract and interrupt you. The women in this anthology are like Ruth; no matter what had come to hinder them from obtaining their promise, they were determined to remain committed to the process to get to the end.

Dr. Essie McKoy, an award-winning educator and a bestselling author, received her Doctorate in Education (Ed.D.) and an Educational Specialist Degree (Ed. S.) from the University of North Carolina at Greensboro, a Master's Degree from Appalachian State University, and a Bachelor of Science Degree from Winston-Salem State University.

She is the President and CEO of her own Educational Consulting Business, Dr. Essie Speaks. Dr. McKoy is a published author and travels the nation to do speaking engagements. In addition, she is the Senior Executive Director of the DMV Mastermind Organization and serves as a faculty member at George Mason University! Furthermore, you will see Dr. McKoy once a month co-hosting about educational topics with Dr. Sharon Porter on the, "I Am Dr. Sharon Show." The segment is entitled, "Education First."

Dr. McKoy has received many awards and accolades for her service in the field of education. Please visit her web site at www.dressiespeaks.com.

My Virtuous Journey

DR. ESSIE MCKOY

"She will never make it in college." These words echoed to my father as he shared with some of his colleagues about me attending college after high school. If I had listened to those who had no belief in me, I would not have acquired four degrees; led a successful, award-winning educational career; attended leadership programs at some of the most prestigious colleges and universities across the nation; or had the opportunity to walk into my destiny of making a greater impact by starting my own business. I would not be a two-time bestselling author, motivational speaker, leadership coach, international radio show host, or a college professor—but God's favor made it all possible!

You see, purpose was already establishing itself in my life, but I had no idea. My parents worked hard and taught me and my siblings to work harder, go to school, get a good education, and do what is right. I recall those early experiences where I had to serve in many different leadership roles even at a young age. Little did I know that purpose was being designed, my journey was starting, and my destiny was in its infancy stages.

Interestingly, my parents shared some of the virtues that I still live by today, and my purpose is to share some of those life lessons and golden nuggets to positively impact your life.

These lessons and virtues include possessing faith, respecting myself and others, training and teaching others, seeking to be healthy and creating balance, serving mankind, being knowledgeable and gaining wisdom, being resourceful, sharing and spreading love, creating an inviting atmosphere, using time wisely, and developing strong character traits. All these virtues have been evident in my life and career. The first profound life lesson is to always remember to never give up on your dream or your goals—no matter how long it may take or how difficult the journey may become. Just keep going!

As I reflect back on my life, especially when I was young, I think about the many times I served as a Sunday school teacher, a secretary, a delegate at conventions, and a Vacation Bible School teacher; sang in the choir; provided Youth Day messages; shared reports; and fulfilled many church related responsibilities. These were the makings of who I am today! These early life experiences prepared me to walk into any room with confidence, wisdom, grace, and poise. The lesson learned is to be "me," to love the person I was evolving into, to be superior in my mindset, to garner respect while being humble in my approach, and to seek opportunities to better myself.

There were many lessons I learned by making mistakes and failing time and time again. I always believed if you fail, you should get back up and try again until you have reached your goals. Also, there were impactful lessons I learned along the way, and one of the most important lessons was to use failure as an opportunity to become greater than before. My parents told me to try over and over until I succeed. This powerful lesson is one that I continue to practice today. My parents taught me how to work through challenges, how to look at my life as a blessing, how to help others, how to give back more than what was given to me, and how to maximize my potential by honing my skills even at an early age.

From those very humbling days of growing up in the eastern part North Carolina to where I am presently, I vividly remember lacking many of the things I desired. Later in life that taught me another invaluable lesson: It does not matter where you grow up or what your parents may or may not have, but it is the belief that you can still attain goals and be as successful as you so desire.

That desired success is truly an internal belief that is defined by each person. Everyone has their own definition of success that lies in the inner core of their soul. However, the world tends to place attainment of material and financial wealth as indicators of success, but success is far more than what one can attain. Through learned life lessons, I have come to realize that success is truly how you assist others in reaching their potential, how you give back, how you make an impact in the lives of others, and the legacy you create.

Ask yourself – how are you enriching the life of someone else? For me, I am humble and grateful that I have spent my entire adult life making an impact in a field where the beginning of all dreams come true. That is the noble field of education. I truly believed the saying, "I was born to be an educator," and later I added through my life's work that I was born to make an impact.

Growing up in a small town allowed me to be immersed in a concept where the entire community helped to raise all the kids in the neighborhood. The community truly lived out their beliefs about giving back and helping others. Of course, as a child, I was able to witness and emulate this. It became second nature for me to operate in the mindset that there are more blessings to give than to receive. Thus, yielding the life lesson to give and it shall be given unto you. Do not look for a handout but seek how you can reach back and give back. Your blessing will be in the giving.

As I recall, many of the adults in my community did not finish high school, but my parents always told me about the importance of making a better life for myself. In my neighborhood, the importance of family was conveyed, raising kids was a focal point, and again everyone in the neighborhood helped to "raise" me. So I was fortunate to get good advice from all the elders and people of such great wisdom. At the time, I was not happy about the neighbors trying to correct me or give me advice, but looking back, I am thankful. They poured into me the foundational components to make me the best person I grew to become. A lesson learned from this is to listen, take the advice of others, and tuck the advice away until the time is needed to use it.

Interestingly, I truly did not know the impact of my parents not finishing high school until much later in life. I thought they finished school since they would always help me with my homework. I guess they faked it until I made it! This taught me another life lesson: You can speak dreams into other people while you may not have your own dreams become a reality. My parents were an example of this. They made sure I verbalized my dreams even though they were not able to live out their dreams. I remember my late mother telling me if she had finished high school and entered college, she would have majored in nursing. You see, she did not have the opportunity to go to college, but she was able to reap the joy and satisfaction of me finishing high school and going on to receive four degrees. Unfortunately, she passed away right after I received my doctoral degree.

My educational journey allowed me to receive my bachelor's degree in special education. Toward the end of seeking my degree and completing my student teaching, I accepted a position at an alternative middle school and that experience simply changed my life and the trajectory of my career path.

Here I was, young and inexperienced, at an alternative middle school teaching students who were placed there because they could not function in a regular middle school setting. These students were in three to four middle schools before arriving at this alternative school. Their issues were massive, and their challenges were great, but this is where I truly learned to connect, build relationships, and make a difference based on what my parents had taught me. This experience taught me so much about myself, about impacting others, and about me living in my purpose. This is where all the life lessons, values, morals, and ability to persevere became solidified. This was my reality! It was an experience that left a lasting impression on me and gave me the fortitude to seek more education in order to make a greater impact. The students taught me more about life and about things that a textbook could not teach me! Lesson: Difficult situations or experiences can lead us to a place where we would have never gone, and it creates a part of us that we would have never known.

My next career move allowed me to go to a "regular" middle school, where I taught at all levels. What was so interesting about this experience was that it allowed me to gain more experience while I kept my mind on the students who were at the alternative middle school. I recall traveling to work each day and thinking about the impact I could and needed to make with students who had such a challenging time in life and had factors that would impact them in a negative way. Some referred to these students as at-risk, but I use the terminology at-promise. The mindset and passion I possessed allowed me to continue to walk in my destiny. It validated my desire to make a powerful impact in the field of education. Another lesson: First experiences can have a lasting impact and can help create the passion you possess and the journey you may take, as well as give you the foundational skills that may catapult your life or your career.

After serving as a teacher at two middle schools, I decided it was time to transition to a position where I could make a greater impact in the lives of many more students. So I went back to school to seek another degree and credentials so I could become a school administrator. I became an assistant principal at a highly impacted school—again, another experience that magnified my love and passion for working with students who needed the most services and the most human connection!

During the time I served in this role, it gave me an opportunity to gain in-depth perspectives about students who were not only academically challenged, but also environmentally, emotionally, socially, and psychologically challenged.

The needs were so great that the school had a health center on campus. It had a medical doctor, nurse, and other medical professionals to assist students and their families. I learned so much, not only from the professionals providing services, but also about myself, my leadership abilities, and the concept of "tough leadership." I was the assistant principal and had to address a lot of the discipline issues. So I faced unhappy parents and had to learn how to share authentically about their children, render consequences for infractions, and find ways to have all parties walk away with a level of respect and understanding. Indeed, this was a 'make it or break it' experience. I made it and it made me not only a stronger leader, but a stronger person, who was able to confront some of the most challenging issues in some of the most challenging circumstances. An amazing lesson learned is when you face tough situations, it allows you to either stand up and address them or fold and walk away. I stood and stood stronger! As I look back on this experience, I know that it prepared me for some of the most rewarding, but more challenging opportunities ahead!

My next experience gave me the chance to serve a school that no other sitting principal wanted to serve. So I applied and got the position to lead one of the largest Title 1 schools in the district. By now, I knew that I loved to take on challenges such as this. I always found myself going into some of the toughest positions. Lesson: I believe that if you do not extend yourself and your capabilities, you will not get to the core of who you really are and how you can really make a profound impact. Sometimes, you need to deplete yourself before you can find your hidden strengths. You must explore the unknowns about yourself, put yourself to the test, and hunker down when you see no light at the end of the tunnel.

This position was initially a challenge but became a blessing! Many believed that the task was too big and the impact I needed to make was too great. As a new principal, I was excited and ready to prove the naysayers wrong. I wanted this school to become one of the best schools and worked hard to spread the vision to others so they would desire to join the team to make an impact like no other. Well, after several years of living the vision and implementing the mission, we made history by making a huge impact and became a school with the highest growth and received recognition as a Piedmont Signature School despite all the significant obstacles faced. Lesson learned: The story can be written one way, but you have the power to rewrite the ending to yield a successful outcome.

Many times in life we think we can predict or know the outcome before we even begin the journey. Another lesson is to do what you are passionate about, surpass your own goals and expectations, and have faith in the process of what you are trying to accomplish.

Believe it or not, after serving that school for almost seven years, I had a calling on my life to go to another elementary school, where I served the same community as when I first started teaching. I called the sitting superintendent at the time to ask if I could meet with him. So I did and shared with him a vision that had come to me while driving to work to the other school. During the time of the vision, I was not thinking about the other school or having any thoughts about moving to a new school. The vision was so vivid, I knew I had to act on it! This was a "calling on my life" position that I had to accept!

Interestingly, God suddenly spoke to me and said, "You do not have to worry about who is going to this school; you are going." I thought, *What in the world? If this is you, God, I need a sign.* Well, he gave me the sign! As you know, when you ask God or God tells you to do something, He will provide, and this time was no different! This was not a notion or a map to greater success, but an opportunity for me to act in my true calling. Amazingly, this second school became a Piedmont Signature School, one of the highest growth schools in the district. At this time, I had transformed two schools, and I knew it was only God working through me to do the great work that had been done!

Now that I had succeeded in transforming two schools at the elementary level, it was time for me to stretch myself again and take on a bigger challenge. So I negotiated a new assignment where I started the process of transforming a middle school and was able to increase the growth index by 4.72 in two years. That was another sign of the impact of allowing God to use my abilities to assist some of the most challenging schools and most challenging students. Lesson learned: Yield your ways to God and allow Him to work in your life.

Sometimes we think we know what we can do and what is best, but God always has the best master plan.

Currently, I yield to God to continue to design the outcome of my future, allowing Him to use me to make a significant difference in the field of education and in the lives of others. He has given me the opportunity to serve in higher education yet again, to speak in places I had no idea of visiting, to write bestselling books, to be aired all over the country and world, to be highlighted in some of the most renowned magazines, and to continue to coach others to greatness. He has put me in some high places, connected me to some extraordinary people, and given me the opportunity to do some amazing things and travel to new territories. I look at the future with a grand vision, a multitude of new aspirations and bigger and bolder dreams. Lesson: God's promises for your life will come to pass. Believe, have faith, work hard, and allow Him to guide you!

Throughout my journey, this process of serving others has given me the character, courage, wisdom, and strength needed to turn the impossible to possible based on the many successes I accomplished as a leader. Too often in life, we allow our fears to prevent us from moving forward. We become complacent and secure ourselves with boundaries where we limit our abilities and stifle our creativity. We hinder our aspirations and diminish our dreams. Lesson: Do not allow fear to smother your hidden talents and your undiscovered potential. You never know what experience might cause you to leap into your destiny to walk the path that was specifically laid out for you.

Some of the ultimate life lessons I encourage you to embrace are: No matter what you do, just keep moving forward and allow God to order your steps, direct your path, and give Him the honor and glory for you walking in your purpose. Live life to the fullest, garner every experience as a piece to the puzzle, let go of what you think you should become and become what God is designing you to be, and listen to that inner voice—allow it to stir your soul and move your aspirations beyond your own imagination. Dare to be the best you, to be the original and unapologetic you, and to be crafted from an unquilted cloth where you design the pattern. Serve with purpose, make an impact, be exceptional, and inspire and change the lives of others. Leave your legacy!

....

"So Christ himself gave

the apostles, the prophets,

the evangelists, the pastors

and teachers"

(Ephesians 4:11, NIV)

....

Charlene Harrod-Owuamana is a Best-selling Author, Professional Speaker and Educator to youth in Baltimore City, where she started her business as a "Kid's Coach" for her personal Brand "Nursz's HIVE & CEO/Founder of Owuamana Enterprise, LLC.

Nursz's HIVE, inspires youth from ages 8 to 24 years old - to focus on a Career in Healthcare. She teaches and educates the youth to prepare them for their future. She has been in the Healthcare System for over 32 years. With 18 years as a Licensed Practical Nurse (LPN); she graduated from Baltimore County Community College (Essex Campus) with an Associate of Science Degree.

Charlene serves on several boards in her city such as: Black Girls Vote (BGV), Maryland Board of Nursing (CNA Advisory Committee), DMV Mastermind Group and Keeping It Safe & Smart (K.I.S.S.); where she holds several board seats. She has been published in Entrepreneur 2018, Washington D.C. Edition by Trends and Empowering. She has numerous accomplishments to include: Speaking at "Baltimore in Conversation" on Trust VS Mistrust in

Healthcare with the LGBTQ community; two-time Speaker at "NursesTakeDC"; Former founder of Black Nurses Rock – Baltimore Maryland Chapter, where she changed lives by educating the communities in which she served. She is the author of seven books.

Despite all the challenges that her city has been faced with over the years, she returned to the neighborhood where she was raised, after 40 years, to strengthen the Healthcare System and show the community her commitment and dedication. She managed to collaborate with top city leaders and educators; such as, the Baltimore City Mayors Office, Baltimore City Fire Department and others. She has remained busy in vulnerable communities doing what God intended her to do, be nurturing, caring and an inspiring Nurse.

I AM A NURSE!!

My Mom's Death Saved My Life

CHARLENE HARROD-OWUAMANA

In loving memory of Elizabeth "Dorothy" Fullard

Some may ask, "Why would one think that a death saved their life?" Not to mention it was their mom's death. Sometimes we can look at things on the bright side, as if they really have a true meaning. Over the years I have become very interested in why bad things happen to good people. My mom was my everything. So, as you read this chapter, think back to the time you spent with your mom, sister, aunt, loved one and family member. Ask yourself, "What if my loved one's death saved my life? Would my life be different? Would my life be the same?" These are the questions I have been battling for years.

Growing up in a vulnerable community is not easy. It takes a lot of hard work, studying, and a village to help raise a child. You see, when you have been told that you will not succeed in life because of your economic background or your community, you begin to believe what you have been told. But when you have a praying family and neighbors that believe in your potential, you work harder to prove the naysayers wrong. Becoming successful is another challenge that young African Americans face. However, as long you have one person to believe in your success and you put in the work, success is possible and life can be amazing.

When I think back over my childhood, I sometimes wonder why God saved me. Once I had time to focus on my life, it became clear to me why my life was spared. Being raised in Baltimore, MD in the 60's was the best of the best times I shared with my family and friends, living in Lexington Terrace project (770 West Saratoga Street on the 10th floor) for over 13 years before we moved to a five-bedroom house a couple of miles away from what I knew as home. Wow, that was a drastic change from what I was used to. I had to make new friends and was heartbroken to leave my old friends and neighborhood.

We had to move when my mom became the care provider for our grandfather and his sister. Living in the projects and now looking at my current life makes me know that folks who have minimum resources manage to make it out of poverty and make do with the cards they were dealt.

What I can remember from being in the projects was we lived 770 West Saratoga Street on the 10th floor, apartment number 1004. Living in the projects back in the day, on the 10th floor, was not for me. I would walk up all 10 flights because I'd had an incident of being stuck on the elevator. Therefore, I would walk up the steps instead. It didn't help that I was afraid of heights. Who would have believed that a person who lived on the 10th floor of an apartment building would be afraid of heights? Yes, it had been a fear for me, as an adult as well, until my 50th birthday when I decided to rappel off a fifteen-story building. That was challenging for me – I have now overcome my fear of heights by rappelling not once, but twice in two years: a fifteen-story building and a twenty-eight-story building. I must say, it was the most beautiful experience I have ever had and most rewarding to be able to overcome my fear. When I was on top of both buildings it was the first time I ever heard my city, Baltimore City, quiet, and it felt so good. I was in awe of the calm blue sky, and the bright, brilliant colors throughout the landscape of the city. It was so amazing. This wonderful city showed off its colors and calmness, just from my being at the top of the city's tallest buildings. It brought happy tears to my eyes and gave me peace. I know my city has many success stories that show what Baltimore City stands for throughout the world. As I rappelled down the side of the building, I took in the scenery and was amazed that I had just rappelled down a building. I lived to tell my story.

Despite the crime, drugs and abuse reported by the press, this city is rich in education, industry, and most of all, an excellent health-care system.

Living in a building that housed many low-income families, we had formed strong relationships with each other. You see, back in the day, you didn't have to lock everything up. Most families assisted each other. We would sleep outside in the summer on what we called ramps. Back then air conditioners were not widely used and/or some families couldn't afford them. My friends and I used to play with dolls, jacks, bat-n-balls and even play "it's" and jump rope. Those games were inexpensive and most of the time we were taught how to make these things out of household items. We spent a lot of time outdoors. The playground had equipment that worked. We went to recreation centers where we learned to make crafts, had modern dance classes and attended life experience classes. Those were the good old days.

When I attended Lexington Terrace Elementary School, I already knew I wanted to be a doctor or nurse. But back then I didn't see many nurses or doctors that looked like me. That made me more determined. At the clinic I went to, University of Maryland on Redwood Street, I can remember seeing one African American nurse. As I sat there waiting for my visit, I always prayed that she would call my name. I believed she would every time I went to that clinic. I would always let the nurse know that I wanted to be a nurse or doctor. She would answer all my questions and explain everything I needed to know about her profession. For Christmas, I would always tell Santa Claus I wanted a doctor/nurse bag, so that I could always make my family healthy and have a smile on their face. That was the way I felt when I went to the clinic. I was such a great help to my mom while she was caring for my grandfather and his sister. I had a wonderful time talking with my grandfather about the war and how my family came to Baltimore City to live. They lived downtown, where Camden yards is now located. It's amazing how a city can change its look and population.

Getting back to Santa Claus, I believed in Santa Claus for a long time, and my parents were so excited to see my Christmas list, because it always had the same items:

- Two dolls;
- Nurse/Doctor bag;
- Church clothes/shoes/gloves;
- Books, new church purse;
- Play food and tea set.

My childhood was filled with happiness and love. We were a family and our relationships were real. Everyone looked out for each other. I joined First Mt. Olive Freewill Baptist Church, located at the corner of Saratoga Street and Fremont Avenue in Baltimore City. I was baptized at eight years old and attended church every Sunday and Thursday night for Bible Study. I was very active and excited about the love I had for God, not to mention I was on the usher board. I can remember wearing my pink flowered dress with pink stockings to match and let me tell you, I had several pairs of white gloves that I would wear to church. I was like the replica of the first lady of the church. I observed her clothing and the way she presented herself in the church and I knew I had to dress the same way. My mom would make sure that I had church clothes and I had three pairs of shoes (a pair of white dress shoes, black dress shoes and school shoes) and of course, every kid had play shoes and tennis shoes. I believe that being brought up in the church played a valuable part in my life. It taught me discipline and how to respect others and myself. I owe it all to my mom for keeping me grounded.

During my high school days, I was given more responsibilities, at school as well as at home. Before I went to school, I had to clean my room and be sure my bed was made, and all clothing was placed on a hanger. When I came home, I had chores that needed to be completed: dishes and sweeping the kitchen and dining room. I had to be sure that the table was set, as well with clean, dry dishes and glasses. This was preparing me for responsibility and the routine of how to clean up, do my homework when I get home, and prepare for the next day.

I was excited to go to the library on Hollins and Payson Streets. When I was in high school, I was popular, so I had many friends. I would meet my friends after I completed my chores. We would go to the recreation center and/or library, where we made clay ashtrays and pictures by tracing our shadows. During these activities with my friends we were forming bonds with each other. We also were setting goals and planning our future. I was always the teacher and talked with everyone about their future goals. I would stay in contact with my friends during and after high school to be sure they were on track with their goals. But once I moved, I lost contact with some of my friends.

The most difficult time for me while in school was, I wanted to take nursing and that trade was full so I had to go with my second choice, which was Commercial Food Services. It was not what I wanted, but I completed the course as if it was my first choice. I won second place in the State of Maryland High School Cooking Competition. My family and neighbors were so excited the day I came home with the bronze metal. It provided me extra resources to be able to live out my goals.

My last year of high school was the most challenging for me to complete. October 1984 would be the last lesson I would learn from my mother. When she told me to go down the street, that everything would be all right, and then she walked away from the window, I knew in my heart that she didn't want me to observe the house burning down. As a result of a house fire, my younger sister broke her right arm and had a head injury; she was diagnosed with Bell's Palsy (a sudden weakness in the muscles on one half of the face). My older brother was burned over 60% of his body and I fractured both ankles and had a lower back injury that left me with a back brace from the back of my head to the bottom of my buttocks, and was in a wheelchair for several months, and on crutches even longer. At one point they told me I would never be able to walk and run. But when my family prayed for our healing, our prayers were answered. Almighty God stepped in, helped my baby sister and released her from the Bell's Palsy. But the greatest gift was the healing of my brother's burned skin. All the time I was not worried about myself, although it was a long, hard process for me—months of therapy and pain. But to this day God blessed me to be able to walk, run and jump with little to no deficiency. Healing took place on the outside, but we were all broken on the inside from the hurt and pain. It was challenging for all of us, knowing this was going to be the last memory of my mother and younger brother that we would have to remember forever.

My mother and younger brother went to be with the Lord. At that time my family consisted of my older brother Kenneth (16 years old), younger sister Dawnkia (18 months old) and baby brother (Melvin six months old). My older stepsister Deborah (17 years old) used to visit and spend time with our family as well. She was not with us on that night of tragedy for our family. We were a tight-knit family.

Yet again, I had to move. Thanks to my mother's brother and his wife, Samuel and Alice Fullard, for looking after me and my younger sister after the death of our mom. They had one daughter Chantell, who was excited that we came to live with them, because she was an only child. And now she had siblings in the house to talk and play with her. So I would like to personally thank my family for stepping up to the plate and providing a lifestyle for my family. My brother went to live with his friends but we kept in contact on a daily basis. My heart was broken yet again to be separated from my older brother, because my mom told my brother that he had to protect me and now that protection was so far away.

I had dreams of going to college and moving my family out of the neighborhood but instead I was moving out of the neighborhood without the one who had been my biggest supporter. It was difficult for me to handle. I was angry with God, because he had changed my future yet again. I completed one and a half years of Pre-Med, until I thought about how much I no longer cared about my goals and future because I had to go it alone. It was so heartbreaking. I could not sleep at night; I was telling myself that I had moved away and that my mother and brother moved to another state and that I couldn't afford to take the trip to see them. Sometimes we tell ourselves something so much we begin to believe it.

I went into Computer Programming, and yet again I proved to myself that I was going to do the best I knew how, and I succeeded. I found a nice job working with the State of Maryland, making pretty good money and a future for myself. Shortly after I started my career, I got married and was married for 22 years. I had a wonderful family and career. Those were the best years of my life. I was able to get the medical attention I needed to escape the depression that I was in for so many years. Being depressed plays a critical role in our lives. If we are not treated and cared for during that time of need, we will be lost and it will be hard to find our way back. But again, I had a praying family that prayed for me and kept in contact with me to be sure I was seeking the assistance I needed. My friends did not know that I was not as strong as I appeared to be. It took me years to get on the right medication regimen to be able to function. It was a long and lonely road at times. I had been going through so many changes and all those moments that I thought I had it together were a mere picture. It wasn't until I looked back on my life that I had to start thanking God for all his gifts, being obedient and following his way, knowing and praying to him when I was in need, and thanking him for the times that I did not think I needed him.

When I would visit the old neighborhood, I could not find my friends. It was as if I had moved from my neighborhood and lost my friends again. After a couple of years, I went back to the neighborhood again. What I saw was heartbreaking. My friends no longer looked the way I remembered them. They were no longer focused on their goals and the plans we made. It was almost as if they were trying to avoid me. It was so confusing to me at first. The biggest reason they were avoiding me was because of their new lifestyle. They felt embarrassed to let me see them, for me to know that they had turned to using drugs and other activities as well. They all knew that I had become a nurse and was doing well for myself. I found out that when they knew I was in the neighborhood they would either go in the house and/or leave the neighborhood until I left the area. But one day, I knocked on their doors and stayed in the neighborhood longer than usual. I had to have a long conversation with them to let them know that I would be their friend forever, no matter what they did. If they got to the point, they really needed help, I would be there for them, to assist them. I would even assist them with finding employment and housing if need be, because when we were younger, we were all in the same neighborhood with the same dreams. But I guess I had a family and an angel fighting for my safety.

It is not easy going back home to the neighborhood you know and seeing that it has changed. You go blocks and blocks and see that the dynamics have changed. There are so many empty houses and different people that I feel lost in my own neighborhood. It saddens me to know that this community has changed in a drastic way. Some of my best friends have been killed and/or took their lives. Sometimes it really plays tricks on my mind to know that there's nothing that I can do to change the trajectory. The one thing that they can't take away from me is the prayer that I pray to God to fix my friends and myself. When two or more pray things really happen for the best. I'm optimistic about a shift in their lives and mine. I also tell them that I am no different, because we all have our own lives and if you seek to change, you must want it.

In conclusion, my mom's death saved my life because I moved away from the crime and drugs that ran fast through the only neighborhood that I called home. They do not discriminate as to whom they befriend. They have no specific color and/or address. They take the weak and vulnerable. They work on the young and the old generation. They consume children, women and men. If you try them, you will continue to chase the feeling. It may even be that some people do not know how and/or never had anyone to tell them "I LOVE YOU." So for my old neighborhood, I want tell all the community of 21223, I LOVE YOU and I do believe we can do better as a VILLAGE, because it takes a village to raise a family. That goes for all of us. Thanks for letting me come back home and to be able to care for the only community I know: WEST BALTIMORE!

Cynthia Greene is a Marriage and Relationship Visionary and Strategist. This dynamic speaker is unstoppable, on a mission and makes no apologies for the destiny that she is on to reignite, redesign and reshape the way the world thinks about relationships and marriage. Cynthia Greene wants to 'Show' the world that there are great relationships out there and everyone can have one!

Cynthia is Founder and CEO of Marriage Built 2 Last, LLC. She is a Certified Professional Life Coach, Certified Prepare & Enrich Facilitator, Entrepreneur, Philanthropist, two time Best Selling Author and Speaker. She has been featured in The Huffington Post, Our Weddings Magazine, a Digital Facilitator at the Power Networking Conference and speaker at Black CEO Black and Influential Conference, 72 Hours of Power, CouplesFest Expo and Festival and much more. Her favorite quote, "If you build it, it will last!"

The Proverbs Virtuous Wife When the Journey Begins

CYNTHIA GREENE

The Proverbs 31 woman is my spiritual 'Shero.' I say spiritual because I have some real life 'sheroes' too. I remember when I first read that entire verse my first thought was, *nobody can meet up to that!* I also remember that back in the day many women felt that way. There was a lot of talk about how she was presented as this superwoman that was impossible for any woman to measure up to. Some may still feel that way.

Today women have become more comfortable in who they are and they realize all too well the many facets of a woman who doesn't always have it all, but she knows that she can do, and be, anything that she sets her mind to. This is where I would say that I am today. I believe that I can do anything that God says I can. I can also say that I am at a place in my life where I am open to a life-long mission to 'DO' all that I am purposed and called to. No goal, dream, idea, or mission is too small or too big.

Let me be clear: I used to be a little intimidated by the 'Virtuous Woman.' But there came a time in my life where I identified with her and, every facet of her story. Today, I identify strongly with the 'Virtuous Woman' (VW). I will attempt to show you how.

Who can find a virtuous and capable wife? She is more precious than rubies.

I cannot truly say that my husband 'found' me as much as I can say that we stumbled upon a friendship. We first met in 1986 when he was in the Air Force and got stationed in my hometown, Fayetteville, NC. For whatever reason, he chose not to stay on the military base and got an apartment in my neighborhood. We became friends through mutual friends. Fast forward 20 years later; we married. The journey from meeting to becoming friends and later marrying prepared me for the lifelong mission that God would place me on to help marriages. It is during that time that I began to identify with the VW and all of her attributes. As I grew in that role, God began to use me.

First, the VW had great faith. Being virtuous meant she had high moral standards. She spoke with wisdom and she feared the Lord. I love the Lord with all my heart, mind, strength and soul. He comes first in my life, before anyone or anything. How, you may ask. Before my feet hit the floor in the morning, I spend the first 30 minutes (at a minimum) spending time with Him, in prayer, worship and meditation. My alarm clock is set to wake me up to start prayer and then it is set during that time for my worship music to begin playing. There is nothing that fuels my inner being or my day more than getting started with a listening ear and an open heart to Him. I pray and consult with Him throughout my day and my life. My faith is what keeps me going in every area of my life and for my family and community. It is important to me that I live a life that the Lord will find pleasing. This helps me to have clarity in planning, preparing and staying on the right path as much as possible.

Secondly, the VW was a great mom, great cook and homemaker. She taught her children with wisdom and kindness; she took great care of the family by preparing healthy meals and making sure they were well dressed. And they blessed her. Our first ministry begins in the home. My family is a blended family.

When we married, we both had two children. We raised our kids totally different. Whereas James was a strict disciplinarian, I believed in allowing my kids to be independent and to be able to express themselves. I raised my kids eating very healthy meals, taking education seriously and being involved in the community. Today I purchase organic and locally grown food for my family. I cook healthy meals and we eat meals together. Our entire family loves every vegetable that grows in the earth and we watch what goes into our body. We strongly believe in health and fitness for ourselves and the environment. What good is our life with wealth in riches in love and family if our health is struggling? We must stay focused and keep this as a priority.

Third, the VW was a wise businesswoman and smart when it came to investing and finances. She worked willingly with her hands. She chose the things that she purchased wisely to make good investments and she used her time wisely to make sure that she completed all of her daily tasks. I worked in corporate America from the time I got out of college in 1984 until the day corporate America laid me off in 2014. From that day forward I had to make a conscious decision how I would manage the rest of my life. One day God told me that I was not called to a j.o.b. I started my own business and never looked back. I have had to learn how to manage my business with care and wisdom so that as I make money, I reinvest that money to grow the business and myself professionally and personally. I have learned what it is to be a solopreneur and what it is to build a team to support me in my dreams and endeavors. I know that it takes hard work, commitment and focus to be successful in business. I make sure that I seek wise counsel, training and support in my endeavors. At times, it is difficult, but with prayer and the support of those who believe in me and my mission, I keep going. I have learned that collaboration and partnership are key.

Fifth, the VW took care of herself and those around her. She paid attention to what she (and her family) wore; she kept herself physically healthy and strong. She was a woman of worth and beauty. Most times, we as women we don't pay attention to how we are nurturing and growing and examining ourselves. Are we kind, friendly, giving, caring, selfless? Do we consciously take care of our health? For self-care, I love to spend time listening to live jazz. I love taking a whole morning or afternoon to wash and style my own natural hair. I go walking and do short spurts of jogging most weekday mornings. I think that it is important to make my health and the way I look a priority. When we take care of ourselves, we are much more able to care for others.

And last but not least, my favorite, the VW was married and a great wife. The Bible says that she was a capable wife, her husband trusted her and she greatly enriched his life. She brought him good, not harm; she got up early and cooked his breakfast. Her husband praised her. After the Lord, my husband is my pride and joy. Not only am I married to the love of my life and am crazy in love, after almost 12 years, I am still on my honeymoon! Now I know some people can't fathom that but it's okay. God knows. Not only do I get to do life together with him but we run our business together. And I truly believe that because we learned to do marriage the way God's word said, He trusted us to help others in marriage. I love when hubby wakes me every morning before going to work to pray with me and kiss me goodbye. I love that I get the opportunity to cook him home-cooked meals, his preference to eating out. I love that we both love quality time together and our favorite pastime is anything that we are doing together. I love that we are like two peas in a pod and love most things alike.

I do not believe that being a VW means that you can do all things and that you are all things. What I do believe is that EVERY woman can be a VW and fulfill her destiny in the world. When she relies on God, believes His words are her instructions and follows them and carries them out, she can live in purpose and in His will. She can attain every dream and desire that God has in store for her. You can best believe that if her husband, children or others around her are praising her, the rest of the world will too.

I am walking in my calling and marching along in my destiny. I make no apologies about fulfilling everything that God has called me to fulfill as a woman, a wife, a mother, a friend, an advocate, a philanthropist, an entrepreneur, a lover of His Word and an anointed wife. As I journey through life, I don't do it alone; I bring my sisters along by supporting them, encouraging them and enlightening them. Currently, I mentor three young ladies in life, business and as a wife to give back.

God showed me my destiny through the power of being a wife. He taught me how to be that virtuous woman (wife) through the 40-day journey that he took me and my spouse on before marriage (Read all about it in our book, *40 Day Journey to the #MarriageOfYourDreams*). My heart and my mission in life are to help eradicate divorce or at the very least, be a catalyst to greatly reduce it. No longer will I stand on the sidelines and watch couples destroy their marriages because of small things that grow into mountains. God's word teaches us what we need to be and how to have the prosperous, joyous life that He pre-destined for us. I want to help others put on that armor that protects us, but also opens us up to the undivided truth and the possibilities of what truly empowers us when we marry and do marriage the way God intended it. When the journey of dating, love, courting, engagement and finally marriage carries you down that path, prep and prepare your entire life, and you will forever be empowered in the joys of matrimony.

Cynthia White Greene, Author, Speaker, Entrepreneur, Coach

"He who finds a wife finds what is good and receives favor from the LORD."

(Proverbs 18:22, NIV)

Dr. Sharon H. Porter, (Dr. Sharon), is an Educator, Best-Selling Author, Publisher, and Interview Host. She has served as an educator for over 25 years as a classroom teacher, Test Development Specialist, Regional Instructional Specialist, assistant principal, Leadership Development Coach, and elementary and middle school principal.

She is a graduate of Winston-Salem State University, National-Louis University, The Johns Hopkins University, Walden University, and Howard University.

Dr. Sharon is the host of The I Am Dr. Sharon Show, a LIVE weekly in-studio interview show, owner of SHP Enterprise Inc., which consist of Perfect Time SHP LLC, Coaching, Consulting, and Book Publishing Firm, The GRIND Entrepreneur Network, Write the Book Now, and SHP Media. She is the Executive Director of the Next in Line to Lead Aspiring Principal Leadership Academy

She is a proud member of Delta Sigma Theta Sorority, Incorporated, International Association of Women (IAW), an Official Member of the Forbes Coaches Council, Sister 4 Sisters Network, Inc., and Professional Women of Winston-Salem.

Be Still and Know...

DR. SHARON H. PORTER

It was January 2018, right at the end of the first month of the new year...My North Carolina family got the news that a cousin (my mom's first cousin on her mother's side) had passed. I remember her coming to visit us often in Winston-Salem, NC. I thought to myself, *Starting the year off with death can't be good.* That was January 16, 2018.

Another call came... January 27, 2018. Another cousin (my mom's first cousin on her father's side) had passed. While I was not close to this specific family member, I knew one of her daughters and a few of her brothers. She was a ROCK to her immediate family and the glue that kept everyone together. Living in Maryland, I was not always able to travel to the various family funerals that occurred in South Carolina and was not able to attend this particular service.

Although my mother and her siblings live in North Carolina, the family really is from South Carolina...Anderson, South Carolina. Both of my maternal grandparents were from South Carolina, so the majority of the larger family still lives there. This cousin who passed had several daughters. I knew only one of them personally. My heart ached for all of them, though. Just a few months prior to this devastating news, a family tragedy occurred. A house fire took three of the daughters' children...Two siblings and a cousin. These deaths were extremely difficult for the family.

June 16, 2018. Death came closer to home. This time it was my uncle, my mother's brother. He was my pastor for my entire childhood and a good part of my young adulthood. His daughters (my first cousins) were more like my sisters than my cousins. My heart ached...not so much for me, but for my cousins. Things began to feel a little different. Our family was not exempt from the loss of family members, but it had been a while. My grandparents were the first family members to leave this world, my grandmother being first. She was a matriarch for our family. After my grandmother was my grandfather, then my dad in 2008. Not long after that was my aunt's husband and first cousin's dad. We knew the sting of death; it was just some time ago since we had actually felt it.

July 22, 2018. My aunt (my mom's sister) passed. Here we go again, just three weeks short of burying my uncle, we were back to grieve for my aunt. My aunt had one daughter and we also were extremely close. In fact, when we were younger, she stayed with us during the summer months. We truly grew up like sisters. She was a few years older and we would become much closer in our adult years than in our childhood and teenage years. Her relationship was strained with her mother, but through it all she loved her mother with everything she had in her. I totally admired her for all she endured. I wouldn't know much of what she went through until she published her first book. She poured her out her heart and soul.

Ironically, her book came out the week her mother transitioned. Our family was doing our best to process all of this grief. Unfortunately, this was not the end of our grieving in 2018.

November 2018, one of my cousins that lived in Maryland had to be rushed to the hospital. It was a Saturday. I was at a networking event and when I received the call, I made my way to the hospital. He was a younger cousin, with a wife and two small children. We have about five or six family members in Maryland, so we try to be there for one another since we don't have a lot of family here. He was having complications from a previous leg injury. He was in the hospital for several weeks. He began to get better. My aunt (his mother) came from North Carolina to help care for him while he was in the hospital. Other family members came to see him while he was on the mend. He began to get better. He was supposed to be released to a rehabilitation center, but he was determined to go home. He had to walk so many steps before the hospital would allow him to go home. He reached the goal and was discharged and was able to go home. My aunt stayed for a few more days. I had plans to travel to North Carolina that week so my cousin asked if I would take his mom back. I said of course and we made provisions to travel to North Carolina.

The next week was Thanksgiving. We always have Thanksgiving service at our church and he was able to attend. About 2 am the Saturday after Thanksgiving I got a call that would send me into a world of uncertainty. My cousin was dead. *What? What do you mean he's dead?* I quickly put on whatever clothes I could find and rushed over to his house. The house was already filled with his wife's family and the many friends and young guys that he mentored. He was still in the house, in his room on the floor. DEAD. I just didn't understand. I was scared, not sure of what to make out of all that was happening. I am a woman of faith, yet I felt faithless. I was confused. My cousin and another aunt had to deliver the news to his mother. He was her only son...her only child. She adored him more than life itself. He was well-known throughout our church in many states. People would come from all over to pay their respects. This was the first time a first cousin that I knew had passed. He was truly like a brother. I was his daughter's Godmother. We were pretty much all we had here in Maryland.

My family in North Carolina chartered a bus for the funeral. It was surreal. Everyone came on the bus except two of my male cousins who had to be back in North Carolina that evening and one female cousin who flew in from Atlanta. She had recently been discharged from the hospital herself. She went to visit her parents in North Carolina for Thanksgiving and ended up having to be admitted to the hospital due to heart complications. She had given birth to a beautiful baby boy almost four months previously. The birth of the baby caused her to have specific heart issues. She felt she couldn't take the bus ride to Washington, DC from Atlanta, so she made arrangements to fly. I would, of course, pick her up from the airport and she would stay the entire weekend with me. She had planned to head back to Atlanta Sunday morning, but I reminded her that my live show was Sunday mornings and I would not be able to get her to the airport until the afternoon or evening. She quickly said, "Oh no, I want to stay for your show," so she made plans to fly out first thing Monday morning.

We had an unbelievable time that weekend. We reminisced about so many things that weekend. Not only did she stay for my show that Sunday, but she was my first ever guest co-host. We had so much fun. After the show Sunday morning, I took her to see the MGM at National Harbor. We had lunch; we talked, laughed, and cried. We were both still just in complete shock at losing our first cousin right on the heels of losing our aunt and uncle.

It was a bit too much. She knew that her heart couldn't take a lot, so she was able to manage all those emotions quite well. She knew how not to get herself worked up. The first cousins had been responsible for the Family Christmas Dinner as well as the Family Reunion in the summer. The cousins were split about whether the Christmas Dinner should occur or not this year. A few did not feel like being festive with all the devastation in our family. Then there were those of us who felt like this was the time that we needed to be together. We were trying to encourage everyone to still plan to be at the Christmas dinner set for Saturday, December 13, 2018 in Winston-Salem, NC.

I took my cousin to the airport on Monday morning, December 10. She was off back to Atlanta. She sent me a text once she landed and told me she had a great time and couldn't wait to return. About 11:45 am EST, Thursday, December 13, 2019 I was having lunch and received a call from my cousin (so I thought). On the other end of the phone, I heard someone I thought was my cousin crying profusely. I shouted, "What is wrong? I can't understand you." I now heard that this was my cousin's husband. He was saying, "She is gone, she is dead." Again, I was not comprehending. "What? What do you mean? What do you mean she is gone, she is dead?" I immediately lost it, right there in the restaurant. I began screaming uncontrollably. I just spent a wonderful weekend with her. I just saw her. I just took her to the airport.

As I write this chapter, "Be Still" by Travis Green is playing on my playlist. How fitting.

Out of all the songs that speak to my heart, this one somehow calms my spirit and lets me know that everything will be ok.

While all of this sadness took place in 2018, the remnants have been felt throughout 2019. There were some days I honestly did not know if I was coming or going. A lot of things suffered, simply because I was not myself. Grief had taken over. I had to pull myself together. My strong network that I would normally lean on (my family) was going through the same devastation as I was. We tried to lean on each other, but truthfully, we weren't much help to each other. We tried. The relationships changed. I felt everyone went into a place of despair.

I felt I didn't even have the support of those I worked closely with over the last five years. It was as if no one cared. In fact, I knew no one cared. About March 2019, I knew I had to find somewhere else to work. This was not the place I was supposed to be. Not long after that, I was called into the Human Resources Office. It was shared that my current position was being eliminated and a new position was being created. I was told I could definitely interview for the new position. It was as if a gray cloud was lifted from my life. I said immediately that I would NOT be interviewing for the new position. It was time to do something else...I wanted to return to the schoolhouse as a principal. This position change would assist me in living out my desired plans for the future.

God has a way of pushing us into what should be, if we only "Be Still and Know."

This devastation has taught me many lessons in this season. I share five of these lessons with you. One thing I will always do is learn the lesson in everything that I do and everything that I go through.

Lesson 1 - Live your life to the fullest. Die empty.

The weekend I spent with my cousin was so special. We talked a lot about all the things she "wished" she could do. I told her, "Girl, you can still do everything you want to do; it's not too late."

I encourage you, don't wait; take action and do what it is you want to do.

Lesson 2 - You must tell people you love them, if you love them.

It's really strange...As close as our family has always been, telling each other we loved each other was not the norm. Somehow, we are now ending all of our calls with "Love you." I'm not sure exactly when it started or even who started, but it has become our "new normal." If you love them, tell them. One day you will not have the opportunity to do so.

Lesson 3 - Self-Care is Health Care.

Do whatever you can to live as healthy as you can. It is selfish not to. We so often forgo the health route for immediate gratification. We don't want to do the extra that it takes or we don't want to let go of certain things. I still grapple with this one. I know for a fact I need to drink more water and leave the soft drinks alone. I know I need to carve out time to exercise. I know I need to make better food choices.

Lesson 4 - Stop seeking approval and validation of others.

I missed out on many opportunities in my life simply because I was fearful of what others would think, say or do. I was trapped. I really feel this is the whole premise of social media. People post things to get "likes" and hearts, etc. I used to be right there, waiting to see who liked my post and how many people liked it. For the last two years or so, I hardly ever go back to a post...It doesn't matter who likes it. I no longer post for likes. I have simply evolved over the last few years. My past experiences have changed who I am.

Lesson 5 - Make Room.

The song "Make Room" by Jonathan McReynolds starts out, "I make time for what I want, I choose my priorities and Jesus you're my Number One, so I will Make Room for You" ...As a Faith Walker, I had to hit the reset button. I found myself caught up with trying to make every networking event, trying to be a part of everyone's books, trying to interview people on my show and all for what? I had pushed God out of my life. I was not making room for Him. The song continues..." Whatever it is, that's not like You…. Move that Over." It's a powerful reminder that when it comes down to it…God is all we have. We have to make room for Him. Actually, He should be FIRST and everything else will come after we have out time for Him. Simply…Make Room!

My two beautiful cousins each left two small beautiful children. This is probably what hurts the most. My cousin in Atlanta's youngest child turned four months exactly on the day she died. He will never know her. I am certain though that through our family, we will make sure he knows who she was and that her boys were her entire world. The same applies for my male cousin who passed in Maryland. His beautiful family is carrying on and making sure his memory stays alive.

After all I've gone through, I know that there will be sunny days and there will also be more days that will bring rain and storms. I will continue to Be Still and Know that He is God. I will continue to cast my cares on Him. I will continue to be a Woman of Virtue Walking in Excellence.

He says, "Be still, and

know that I am God;

I will be exalted among the

nations, I will be exalted

in the earth."

(Psalm 46:10, NIV)

Elder Falecia Michelle McMillian is grateful and honored to be a child of the only true and living God!

She earned her Bachelor of Science in Speech Communications, a minor in English/Journalism, her Master of Science in Curriculum Design and Instruction and she is currently working on her doctorate in Educational Leadership. Elder McMillian has had a myriad of opportunities to share God's love via preaching and teaching at various churches and for various organizations throughout the east coast of the United States.

Elder McMillian is an elementary school Principal and has received numerous awards and commendations for her work as an educator.

She is an abundantly blessed mother of three daughters, all affectionately known as her Q.I.T's –Queens In Training. As a cancer survivor, she knows beyond a shadow of a doubt that she can do all things through Christ who strengthens her -Philippians 4:13!

Perseverance

FALECIA MCMILLIAN

"You are my second daughter...but you're my first daughter to survive." These were some of the most shocking words I've ever heard my beloved mother say. She went on to say, "I was pregnant with a daughter when I lost her on my kitchen floor due to a beating I'd suffered." I gasped and cried as she described the agony she endured. I cried because this innocent life was taken before it began. I cried because I had no idea the pain that my mother went through losing a child at seven months of pregnancy. I cried because I was livid that my sister died and I never got a chance to know her. My mother said nothing as I cried; she let me have my space to process this horrible tragedy.

I stopped sobbing long enough for Mother to continue sharing. She went on to say that the next year, she became pregnant with me. She was happy and hopeful that she would deliver me at full term...without any interruptions...without any threats to her life or mine. She was even more excited to learn that she was having a girl! She'd always wanted a girl and now, God had given her a second chance to have the daughter she'd longed for! "Then, when I was five months pregnant with you, Falecia," Mother went on to say, "I was walking home one day, just a few steps away from my house, when I was attacked...someone started beating me from behind. The beating caused me to fall to the ground. It was broad daylight. People were outside, but no one helped me. When I fell, I curled into in the fetal position and I protected my stomach…I protected you from the blows I was receiving. Over me stood my attacker. I begged him to stop beating me; eventually, he did."

From the time I was conceived even to the writing of this chapter for this great work, my life has been one of sheer perseverance. Perseverance, as defined by Merriam-Webster, is continued effort to do or achieve something despite difficulties, failure, or opposition. My mother was perseverance personified. I was right there, seeing the challenges and the triumphs she experienced day in and day out. She never complained and she took every obstacle in stride. My mother left that same spirit in me—the spirit to persevere, to never give up!

Although I thought I was on my way to becoming the next Oprah Winfrey, God had other plans. I'd earned my Bachelor of Science in Speech Communications and my minor in English/Journalism. To say that my family was proud of me is a tremendous understatement! I was the first in my family to attend and graduate from college. God blessed me to receive a full academic scholarship for college. I wanted to be on television, helping people by providing support and making a "name" for myself.

Nevertheless, God had other plans for my life. His plans included me magnifying His name and not my own. God sent me back to school as He called me to be an educator. God lined things up and although I'd gotten married, moved to Maryland (from Norfolk, VA) and had a baby, I could pursue certification to become a teacher and thus, I did. I persevered as I drove after church on Sundays from my home in Silver Spring, Maryland to Stafford, Virginia to take a mathematics course to qualify me to teach. Simultaneously,

I took reading classes at Prince George's Community College, as these classes were not offered at Strayer College (the college I drove to on Sundays) and I needed these classes as well to secure my teaching certification. While at Prince George's Community College, God allowed me to befriend a young lady who invited me to meet her principal. I had not even completed my courses and yet this lady wanted me to meet her principal?! I pondered that reality for a moment and then I took her up on her offer. I stepped out on faith; I moved in the direction of my destiny. God has given me a faith that works in that I put my plan in place and I work toward that plan. God's Word reminds us that "faith by itself, if it does not have works, is dead." (James 2:17, NKJV).

Within a week, I was meeting the principal, Dr. Yvonne Crawford, who is one of the greatest educational leaders I've ever met. What I thought was a meeting ended up being an interview. I praise God that I was prepared, answering all her questions with precision and clarity. I so impressed Dr. Crawford that she gave me a tour of the school and offered me a teaching position at her school! I was humbled and amazed…excited and nervous…grateful and prayer-ful…all at the same time! Even though I hadn't completed my courses for certification, I accepted the offer to teach first grade. Upon speaking with the human resources department, I learned that I needed to do some additional items in order to start teach-ing…I had to pass three PRAXIS examinations. I easily passed the first examination. Test number two was no problem; I aced it without batting an eye. And then came the third assessment, the mathematics assessment, and let's just say mathematics and I have had our ups and downs! I did not pass the mathematics assessment and while I was concerned, I persevered. Therefore, I took the mathematics assessment for a second time and…I didn't pass it. Here comes the third try and guess what? I didn't pass the exam.

But God told me to fight on and so I did. I began to, like David, encourage myself in the Lord (I Samuel 30:6). The Sunday before I took the exam for the seventh time, my pastor preached a message on determination. My pastor had no idea what I was going through with these exams and he certainly did not know that I was about to take the exam for the seventh time the very next day. My pastor exclaimed, "Don't wait until the battle's over, shout now!" The Holy Spirit came over me and I danced and praised the Lord with all my might. I settled in my spirit that regardless of the test results on tomorrow, God would be praised.

I took the mathematics assessment for the seventh time. At the end of the test, I sat with my head down as I waited for the computer to generate my score. I gave it all I had. I thought about how I studied, prayed, believed God…I thought about how I registered for the test every sixty days, as that was the wait time between tests. I thought about how I wanted to make my mommy proud… how I wanted to one day tell my daughter how I'd persevered and that she would have the same persevering spirit to never give up. I thanked God for yet another opportunity to complete the assessment. Finally, I lifted my head to view my score on the computer screen. "Yes!" I yelled as I looked at the score! The test examiner knocked on the glass and told me to leave the testing room. "You can't make noise in there…you could have your scores disqualified for disrupting the testing environment," the testing manager explained. "Excuse me sir, I didn't mean to cause any harm…I'm rejoicing over what God has done! God just allowed me to ace this test and my score is sooo high, I can teach mathematics anywhere in this country! This was my seventh time taking this assessment. God blessed me to pass it and He alone is to be praised!" The test manager said, "Well praise God! I'm happy for you!" I shouted out of that facility, giving God the glory and honor.

Perseverance, is my middle name. There has never been a season in my life where I didn't have to persevere. My next challenge came when, in September of 2010, I was diagnosed with stage two throat cancer. I'd never smoked a day in my life and what—throat cancer?! The doctors didn't know from whence it came and they gave me an 80% chance of survival. I wasn't dismayed when I got the diagnosis. "Thank you for sharing, but I know that my God is going to heal me 100%! I have so much work to do for God's kingdom and I know He's not through with me yet," I told them. After seven weeks of radiation, in early 2011, I was cancer free. Glory to His name!

My next bout with perseverance came in 2013, as I was going through ordination to be an Elder of the Gospel of Jesus Christ and a divorce, simultaneously. I had a conversation with my pastor and shared with him that I was fine if he decided to withdraw me from the process as I was getting a divorce. He said how he believed in me and that the only way I would not go through with the process is if I withdrew myself. Knowing that the Lord was with me, I moved forward with ordination. Drawing closer to God on one hand and permanently leaving the one that I thought I was to love, honor and obey for life, on the other hand, was extreme perseverance. Often, it felt surreal. I felt like I was having an out-of-body experience. I felt like I was literally in the air looking down on two very intricate, different parts of my life. So, I pressed onward, studying God's word, divorcing my husband, raising my daughters, growing in my profession as an elementary assistant principal and working in ministry…to say that the days were long is a gross understatement!

Yet God allowed June 1, 2013 to arrive—this was the day that I was to be questioned and, if approved, nominated for ordination.

Heart pounding, legs wobbly, palms sweaty, stomach in knots, mouth dry, I stood before my catechizers and other invited clergy for my examination. After what seemed like an eternity, I was given permission to leave and wait for the results from my catechizers. A few days later, the ordination ceremony commenced and I was ordained as an Elder of the Gospel of Jesus Christ! My mother and many others who had supported me along the way were there. One of the greatest highlights of my life was having my mother put my clergy collar on me. And thus, it was "official." I'd worked for years in ministry, never seeking a title, position or promotion, but God, who sees all, had this day planned from the very foundations of the world.

Perseverance…To provide clarity on how I was and continue to be able to persevere, here's what I do:

1. Acknowledge where I am.
2. Determine in my mind that I'm going to reach my goal and win.
3. Move toward my goal and monitor my progress.
4. Trust God every step of the way. Prayer, fasting, studying and standing on God's Word are all musts as I persevere.

I've never encountered a time when I had to persevere where the aforementioned process was unsuccessful. Today, after having buried my mommy, my best friend, three years ago, I continue to persevere with my greatest work—raising my three queens in training. God has equipped me and with my mother, now my Angel up in Heaven, smiling down on me, I persevere toward receiving my doctorate in educational leadership and my certification to become a superintendent of schools. I persevere as I continue my career as an elementary school principal and I persevere as I continue to

From Broken, Bitter, and Poisoned to Healed

TONOAH HAMPTON

"You may be at a crossroads in your life. You may have issues to deal with, people you need to forgive. You can go one of two ways. You can ignore what you now know to be true and keep burying that bitterness in your life, pushing it deeper and allowing it to poison and contaminate you and those around you, or you can make a much better choice by getting it out in the open and asking God to help you totally forgive and let it all go." ~Joel Osteen

In January 2006, I married the man I prayed to God about all my life. He is a protector and provider, who loved me for who I was without having to pretend. While dating, I recall telling him, "I am not Molly the Maid, Suzie Homemaker, or Betty Crocker." It wasn't because I could not do those things. I was capable. It was the result of past experiences with other people. The majority of my youth and young adult days were spent serving others. I was the pastoral staff official babysitter, the personal chef and housekeeper for my family, and the constant lifesaver for countless friends in need. Although those are excellent skills and qualities to possess, I became resentful of serving others, because no one seems to care about my needs. But God has a sense of humor; these skills and abilities to help became the core values of my professional and spiritual assignments. God transformed my brokenness, bitterness, and deadly poison into purpose through forgiveness.

I began my nursing career in high school as a Certified Nursing Assistant, working with the elderly, and later earned several degrees to become a master's prepared Registered Nurse. Countless hours were spent providing care for the elderly, while they shared pearls of wisdom with each encounter. I thought I was helping them, but I would soon realize they were sharing knowledge I needed to survive in the days ahead. Despite being an advocate for health and well-being for others, I failed to extend the same care and compassion to myself. My innermost being was shattered and in disrepair as the result of life's challenges; mistakenly, I believed that marriage to this wonderful man was going to fix everything that was broken or missing.

When I married for the second time in 2006, it was supposed to fix everything. My two children from two previous relationships finally had a father that loved them. Well, it didn't totally go as planned. My children weren't accustomed to having a male figure in their lives. So when I got married, they became extremely jealous of the time I was spending with this new person. My oldest son, Giovanni, took the relationship the worst. He was about 12 years old, and rebellion was the order of the day. He didn't like the discipline or the loss of his mother's attention. Tension in the house became so great that I wanted to quit being a wife and a mother. I threatened to leave on numerous occasions. I told him that he could keep everything we had, including all the children, even the ones he didn't make. I was serious. I didn't want the responsibility of caring for another soul. I barely wanted to live at this point. How had I gotten myself into this mess? I knew I could not leave because I didn't want my younger children to experience the pain of fatherlessness that my older children and I experienced.

We were just two years into this "perfect marriage," and I was ready to call it quits because of the frustration associated with caring for others. The peacemaker has no peace. The skillful nurse who assesses a situation and provides interventions for healing was unable to help her family. The marriage wasn't supposed to go this way. My children were going to be perfect and would love my husband as much as I did. Life was falling apart right in front of my eyes, and I felt so alone. I did not trust anyone enough to share my experiences or feelings. I thought I had to shoulder the weight of this struggle alone, just like all the other times in my life. But I hadn't hit rock bottom just yet.

Early one Sunday morning, the tension in the house reached an all-time high. The sound of yelling and commotion pierced the peaceful silence. The voices of my husband and son echoed throughout our tiny townhouse. I rushed to figure out what all the commotion was about, only to see my son standing on the bed with a pocketknife. He was threatening to kill my husband, and the other children were screaming and crying. The chaos was shocking, and I did not know what to do. I quickly jumped into action to deescalate the situation. But that was short-lived because unknown to me, the police were en route to my house. My husband told me I had to make a choice; someone was leaving. This ultimatum rocked me to my core. Who do you choose? I gave birth to my son and loved him immensely. But I loved my husband, and we had two children together. The children needed their father. Big, bad, I-want-to-leave-Tonoah wasn't so big and tough at that moment. I wish I could say that I prayed, but I didn't.

Upon the police's arrival, they instructed us that even though he called, he faced being arrested and taken to the juvenile detention center. I couldn't let him become a part of the system because of a misunderstanding. He only wanted the love and attention of his mother. I made a life-changing decision. My son went to live with his father. However, his father quickly sent him away. He felt rejected and abandoned by his father and me. This abandonment by his father further separated me from my son and created a deep wound in both of our hearts. I became depressed, with feelings of failure and utter despair. However, I was forced to put on a mask for everyone else to attempt to protect my heart and hide my pain.

Physically, spiritually, and emotionally wounded, I was dying. I started hemorrhaging on the inside. Month after month, I became weaker and weaker from the loss of enormous amounts of blood with my menstrual cycle. I began to experience sickness after sickness, including abdominal pains, fatigue, and tumor growth. I thought the tumors were simply fibroids that are common in women. Despite being a nurse, I choose to ignore the consequences of not addressing my health. The loss of my son created utter pain that compounded my health issues.

Eventually, I was forced to address my health concerns. My health deteriorated to a level where the doctors stated that I needed to make some decisions before my body did it for me. Since the fibroids seemed to be the culprit of many of the issues I was experiencing, I agreed to have a hysterectomy to address the problems. However, the problem persisted, and my mental and emotional health began to fail. As I fought bouts of depression and anguish over the absence of my son, the pain increased. The tumors continued to grow even without a uterus. Throughout my abdominal cavity, tumors continued to grow, some as large as grapefruits.

They were on my intestines, liver, and bladder. In 11 years, I would undergo 11 abdominal surgeries to correct a condition the doctor could not explain.

Once again, in 2015, I began to experience abdominal pains. The excruciating pain became overbearing. I began to cry as the doctor explained that surgery was needed again. This time the procedure was going to be more difficult, as the presence of scar tissue from the previous operations would make it risky. The risk was more significant than the last 11 procedures. The mass that was growing on my liver was attached to my intestines. Multiple specialists were consulted to ensure the best physical outcome.

As I prepared for this surgery, I began praying and asking God to reveal the source of these tumors and illnesses. Before surgery, during my prayer time, I did not hear one word. I felt like God had left me alone because of my past choices. But I continued to pray for an answer. I believed that God was the only one that could answer these daunting questions. Throughout my eight-week recovery, I began to hear God speak. Perhaps it was because I finally sat still and wasn't finding other people to entertain me or things to do.

Screenshots of various life events began to flash before my eyes during prayer. I remembered the rejection from my biological father, molestation at age four, lack of affection from my mother, raped by a childhood friend, countless episodes of fornication with people I knew little about, the adultery and abandonment from my first husband, and the loss of relationship with my firstborn son, just to name a few. The traumatic wounds of these events had created disease in my physical body, particularly in the area of my womb. My choices created many of the wounds, while some were the result of other people's actions. I conceded to the lies told to me by the enemy, and I began to act them out without consulting God. These choices led to years of sickness: body, mind, and spirit.

While lying on my recovery bed, I began researching the things showed to me. Research showed scientists have determined that our spiritual health impacts our physical health, and vice versa. The diseases, or should I say tumors, were the result of years of harboring the feelings of rejection, hurt, and bitterness. I engaged in activities that soothed my physical body temporarily, but ultimately became the breeding ground for disease to survive.

The definition of disease is without physical comfort, or disturbed state of body, tranquility, or peace of mind. Disease is the result of internal and external factors that cause pain, distress, social problems, dysfunction, and even death. The factors fall into seven domains: physical, mental, emotional, nutritional, financial, relational, and spiritual health. The seven areas impact health.

So the question to God became what issues did I allow to cause me to "be without physical comfort, a calm state of body, tranquility, or peace of mind, in the seven domains of health?" Was I truly ready to be healed by the Great Physician? I had to engage in my healing actively. I had to assess my entire being through the guidance of God during my prayer and recovery time.

It is reasonable to conclude that I would be lonely, despite being married; isolated; financially challenged, living paycheck to paycheck; anemic; and possibly dying physically from cancer, the constant looming diagnosis; and spiritually depleted. My prognosis was hopeless, and I was desperate for a cure. I was willing to risk it all for the sake of living. I had to truly trust the God that I said I love and serve.

"For I will restore health to you, And I will heal your wounds, says the Lord, because they have called you an outcast, saying: 'This is Zion; no one seeks her and no one cares for her.'" (Jeremiah 30:17, AMP)

This scripture became the foundation for my healing. The promise of God to restore health to a nation that had experienced numerous challenges ministered the healing balm to the broken places in my body, mind, and spirit. I had my answer; I needed God to be the life-giving balm that I searched for, for many years in people, things, money, and food. God was the answer. The prescription was a personal relationship with God. Don't get me wrong; I was saved and knew the holy scriptures. I even knew how to pray. However, I did not engage in an intimate relationship with God. I sought intimacy from my husband that I thought would change my life forever. But in an attempt to find security from my natural husband, I failed to maintain an intimate relationship with God that would be needed to traverse the health obstacles that I faced.

Based on the comprehensive assessment of my life through a spiritual lens, God gave me the plan for my healing. If I was going to overcome man's prognosis of loneliness, isolation, poverty, and death, a God-designed comprehensive care plan was going to be needed. I would have to utilize my voice to speak life to my situation and during conversations with my physicians. Despite the medical diagnoses and adverse medical reports, I had to advocate for the incorporation of my spiritual beliefs in my plan of care. No longer was I going to allow the doctors to continue to prescribe medications and perform surgical procedures without my considering God.

During a visit with my medical oncologist in 2017, I decided I was no longer going to take chemotherapy or hormone suppression medications. They were causing extreme muscle loss, weight gain, and further depression. The decision did not sit well with her, and she recommended another surgical procedure to remove the one ovary that I had left. She notified my gynecology oncologist to inform him that I wasn't willing to take the medications any longer and that he would need to perform surgery. I scheduled a telephone appointment to speak with the gynecology oncologist. The most amazing thing happened in the conversation. He stated, "Since there is no research to support that the treatment will prevent the reoccurrence of this rare metastasizing tumor. I recommend that you keep praying. I will monitor you every six months to a year. And we will believe God that they will never return." I was shocked. I never told him that I prayed, or believed God, for that matter.

It was at that moment that I knew that God's plan for my life was to address each area of my health (physically, emotionally, mentally, nutritionally, financially, relationally, and spiritually). But first, I had to be honest with myself and forgive others. Forgiveness became the key to my healing. Forgiving others is not an option. It is the first step in obedience to God and freedom for you. Forgiveness does not mean that the others that hurt me were right or the decisions that bothered me were right, but forgiving provides the freedom to heal.

Several years have passed, and many more health challenges have surfaced, but God has allowed me to experience healing in every area of my life. The most significant area of healing I experienced was in my relational health. Once I was honest about my feelings and how they impacted my choices and relationships, I was able to have an intimate relationship with God. Intimacy with God increased my ability to hear clear instructions for interactions with others, including my husband, son, and doctors. I have found my voice to effectively communicate from a position of love and respect for others while representing Christ on the earth. God restored my relationships with my husband and son, as promised.

The hurts of my past no longer dictate the direction for my future. Disease has been uprooted by the healing power of forgiveness. I now live with physical comfort and a calm state of body, tranquility, and peace of mind. When life challenges present themselves, I consult with God's care plan for my life before deciding my next steps. Deuteronomy 30:15-16, NIV provides this guidance for decision making:

"See, I set before you today life and prosperity, death and destruction. For I command you today to love your God, to walk in obedience to him, and to keep his commands, decrees, and laws; then will you live and increase, and the Lord, your God, will bless you in the land you are entering to possess."

God's plan for your life outlines that which will bring you life and that which will bring you death. Which decision will you make—life or death? I recommend life-producing choices in every area of your life.

Dr. Mary J. Huntley is a wife of 45 years, 4X Bestselling author, and 2X International Bestselling Author which includes her recent self-published inaugural solo project release, Don't Quit. She is a certified master life coach, motivational speaker, licensed counselor with advanced certifications, and a clinical supervisor. She is an international representative, and a certified temperament coach with a counselors' association. She is on a mission to empower others (especially women) to soar above the storm and reach their God given potential. She is grateful for an earned doctorate degree.

She is the grateful recipient of the Deborah C. Offer Bulgin Women of Virtue Walking in Excellence Award, the Prince George's County Governor's Citation Award, and the Anne Arundel County Executive's Citation Award. She has been featured on international motivational speaker Cheryl Wood's Impact the Nation Radio Show and on phenomenal Nicole Mason's Radio Show.

Website: www.drmaryjhuntley.com
Amazon Author Page: www.Amazon.com/author/drmaryjhuntley
Instagram: authordrmaryjhuntley
Facebook: DrMary J Huntley
Twitter: drmaryj_huntley

Called to Serve

DR. MARY J. HUNTLEY

I am truly honored and blessed to be a part of this amazing Women of Virtue Walking in Excellence anthology. When I think of a woman of virtue, immediately Proverbs 31 comes to mind. A virtuous or godly woman is rare, precious to God and others. She greatly contributes to her husband, children, the church, society and the community. She is more valuable than all earthly possessions. The word virtuous or excellent is a term encompassing her exemplary qualities, actions, and attitudes. Virtuous is also a military term, translated as meaning strength or bravery. A virtuous woman is the counterpart of Israel's mighty man. This woman is praised for qualities that she has developed. The value of women to any society, culture, and certainly the church can never be over-empha-sized. And a wife of noble character is the crown of her husband. God's virtuous woman is no slouch. She has significant attributes and characteristics that include godly character, wisdom, courage, strength, integrity, and honesty. She exemplifies the same godly character behind closed doors and when the shades are down as she does in the public's eye. God's virtuous woman is one who is known in the community for her high moral standards; she believes the Bible and, with the help of the Holy Spirit, applies it to her life. She delights in righteousness and seeks to obey Paul's command to "be not conformed to this world" (Romans 12:2, KJV). Relying upon the Holy Spirit, a virtuous woman can present an envious lifestyle to the unbeliever. Ruth could have left Naomi for her own people who did not fear God, but she chose to stay with her mother-in-law, which meant following Naomi's God. A virtuous woman leaves the world to follow Christ, even if it means leaving the good opinion of family and friends. She is priceless and cannot be bought!

A virtuous woman exemplifies wisdom by building and promoting trust and confidence in her husband. According to Proverbs 31:11, NET the heart of her husband has confidence in her, and he has no lack of gain. His soul (mind, will, intellect) trusts her without reservation or anxiety, because she is trustworthy. After 45 years my husband knows that he can trust me. He is an excellent provider. Our finances are deposited into our JOINT accounts. We come together and ensure that the household obligations are met (starting with our tithes). Because he trusts me, I will never deliberately let him down or disappoint him. A virtuous woman fulfills her role as a wife with excellence and not haphazardly. It is a pleasure to have my husband join me for public events because I am honored and blessed to be his wife and "good thing." A virtuous woman leaves no room for her husband to desire a mistress, girlfriend, or a platonic friendship with a female. It is my responsibility to ensure that he lacks nothing of value found in a virtuous woman. A virtuous woman also exhibits wisdom by promoting entrepreneurship while serving as CEO, and she possesses an enterprising spirit. Proverbs 32:13-14, NET says she obtains wool (winter) and flax (linen, summer) and she is pleased to work with her hands. She is like the merchant ships; she brings her food from afar. She has specific goals and objectives and is skilled and capable in her work. There is no hint of laziness in this virtuous woman, who is praised by God. She works willingly with her hands. Wisdom is seen through her preference to work smart; however, she is up for the task when hard work calls. She is not afraid to roll up her sleeves, or to get her well-manicured nails and hands dirty. This virtuous woman is no prima donna or diva! She is not above manual labor. She is honored to be her husband's helpmeet to the "glory of God." She utilizes wisdom and godly creativity to help her spouse meet each family need.

A virtuous woman exemplifies courage, strength and integrity as an excellent entrepreneur. This Proverbs 31 woman is no wimp! She is undoubtedly God's leading lady. She knows how to serve in her assigned lane with laser-focused brilliance. She has the intelligence and business acumen to evaluate property, as well as make sound business decisions. She seeks God's guidance and she honors and consults her husband as the priest of the household before making decisions. Before we moved into our current home, we prayed about our ideal property. I analyzed our financial portfolio to ensure that we were not prematurely embarking upon a major expense. Next we discussed the findings and agreed that God had given us favor. We were very grateful to move into our new home. Every mortgage payment (with extra principal) has been paid in a timely manner as a result of our great God. I kept a vigilant eye on the interest rates and in 2013 we refinanced to an amazingly low rate. Within a few short years we will be mortgage free unless we decide to pay it off sooner. HALLELUJAH!

A virtuous woman appreciates the value of being a servant, as stated in Matthew 20:26: "But whosoever wishes to become great among you shall be your servant." Matthew 20:28 states, "Just as the Son of Man did not come to be served but to serve…" These scriptures epitomize true servanthood and greatness! It is seen in those who serve in their God-assigned lane of excellence. On September 28, 2003 God said to me, "I am sending you to identify with my people. Many have been hurt, many have been rejected, but you must show them that I love them with an everlasting love and that I'll never leave them nor forsake them. Continue to trust me and I will, I shall bring it to pass. Know that you can always depend on me. Have I not said it, is it not so? I'm not a man to lie. You can always count on me." I proceeded to prepare spiritually, educationally and professionally. In fact, I took advanced courses to enhance my arsenal. I prepared to serve in my lane of brilliance with a spirit of excellence. After much hard work and many long hours, I received six advanced certifications in professional counseling. And I also completed requirements to become an international representative and a clinical supervisor for an organization. Under the guidance of the Holy Spirit and equipped with God's word, methodologies, certifications, and training from professionals I felt better equipped to serve "hurting people." Some may call them the overlooked, unnoticed underdogs (a competitor who is thought to be the least likely to win). Many of us know how it feels not to be looked upon favorably because you do not make the cut or fit certain criteria. However, I learned at an early age to trust in God and His process, believe in myself, to work smart as a preference but not to fear hard work when necessary. I also learned that a winner never quits, and a quitter never wins.

Serving my community and giving back is an honor and a privilege. And I am grateful and blessed to serve as the Chief Executive/ Encouragement Officer in Trinity Global Empowerment Ministries, Inc. We are a 501(c)(3) organization whose mission is to educate, enlighten and empower God's people and to help them reach their pre-ordained purpose. We meet with God, our Commander-In-Chief, in the "Situation Room" (Prayer Room) to debrief and make our requests known as we stand in the gap for those in need. I serve as an advocate for those who find themselves in a holding pattern while awaiting their next move toward destiny.

Some of our professional services include relationship coaching, individual counseling, Group Therapy, Marriage and Family Therapy, Death & Grief Therapy, and Crisis and Abuse Therapy. We also provide Temperament Therapy utilizing an awesome tool that yields over 90% accuracy rate, and it allows us to measure the counselee's needs, natural traits, strengths and weaknesses. We get to the root cause of the client's challenges. Then we can individually address the concerns and empower individuals to proceed toward the "runway" as they take the next step toward destiny. It is our goal to continue networking with and providing professional pro bono services to those in need of our services. We also endeavor to speak up and speak out for those whose voices have been silenced by abuse and domestic violence. Most recently I have partnered with a foundation 2,733 miles away to provide pro bono counseling and coaching for the staff who deals with abused women, women sold into sex trafficking and those who have been made to feel less than human and who have very low self-esteem. As a trained marriage mentor, I also serve as an advocate for those who are experiencing marital challenges. I am honored to coach and counsel clients as far away as the United Kingdom. To God be all the glory! However, I wouldn't be able to serve effectively and to fulfill my assignment without the help of some amazing people, namely my husband of 45 years, Dr. Ronald Lee Huntley. THANK YOU for your consistent love and unwavering support. THANK YOU to the network of licensed professional counselors, certified coaches, licensed clinical social workers, clinical supervisors that are a part of my amazing network. I appreciate every one of you!

So as I travel on life's highway, I am always mindful that I need the proper tools in my arsenal—tools such as The Bread of Life, Living Water, Faith, Prayer and God's Plan. It is an amazing sense of fulfillment when I serve in my lane of brilliance while encouraging others. God will allow your name to be spoken in rooms before you show up if you trust the process and serve in your lane of excellence. Proverbs 18:16, NKJV says, "A man's gift makes room for him and brings him before great men." Therefore, as believers we don't have to step on or try to dim someone's lights to try to get to the top. We don't have to treat others less than human to make them look small. Simply discover your gift and serve God's people and everyone with excellence. The right person will notice your spirit and you will find yourself in the position where God has assigned you to serve. Don't allow anyone to call you where you know you are not assigned. Be not weary in well doing, for you will reap in due season. Trust God's process!

Now I know that people don't care how much I know until they know how much I care. Dr. Maya Angelou also reminds us that "people will forget what you said, people will forget what you did but people will never forget how you made them feel." Therefore, I am always cognizant of the fact that my assignment is not exclusively about me. I've discovered that the best way to help hurting people is to meet them where they are, fill the immediate need and gently or gingerly invite them to grow and go toward their pre-ordained destiny or purpose. I can only accomplish that by exhibiting love, humility, and empathy. I must always remember that but for the grace of God the tables could turn, and I would be in need. So I adopt a servitude attitude, remembering that "if serving is beneath me, surely leadership is beyond me, and that he who is greatest among you must first be a servant." Therefore, I am obligated to those who are seeking safe passage along life's highways I have traveled or am currently traveling. There is power in serving and giving back. In the words of Tyler Perry while delivering his BET acceptance speech for the Ultimate Icon Award, "It's all about trying to help someone cross."

I have had the privilege of serving as advocate for students who were stuck in their educational quest. These ladies worked full time jobs and took graduate level courses, in addition to caring for their families. WOW, does this bring back memories, especially since I graduated from night school while working full time during the day. And I completed graduate level courses while working full time. However, when these ladies were challenged and thought that they were ready to quit, I was honored to show up with my arsenal of prayer and a plan to help them reach the finish line. And I was honored to attend their graduations. I continue to serve in the ministry and provide sources and resources for those traveling along life's highway. God recently blessed me to release my inaugural, international bestseller solo project titled *Don't Quit: Motivation To Reach Your Goals*. I am presently utilizing this high-octane motivation to encourage those who feel like giving up. Specific methodologies are included that will help persons crush their goals. I discuss the importance of setting S.M.A.R.T. goals and the importance of each letter. Empowering and helpful tools, motivational quotes, and encouraging scriptures are also included in this powerful book to assist and guide the reader. And the reader can reflect at end of each chapter by answering strategic questions that will help retain this powerful information. To those who are victims of domestic violence, abuse, sex trafficking, and other crises, I am honored to assist and help to ensure that your voice is heard and that you are rescued and protected. To those who have suffered loss, I am professionally trained and honored to serve in the "ministry of presence" to help you through the grief process.

On October 14, 2017 I had the honor and awesome experience of accepting the Deborah C. Offer Bulgin Women of Virtue Walking in Excellence Award. This prestigious award is named after Dr. Tasheka Green's mother, who was a studious, phenomenal,

God-fearing and virtuous woman who lost her life to stage four stomach cancer in 2010. She was an individual of extraordinary vision, talent, presence and accomplishment. She was a born leader and worked tirelessly to ensure that her daughters had whatever they needed to become successful women. I received this phenomenal award for outstanding servant leadership, contributions, and dedication in being a voice in the community to encourage, motivate and push women to their goals, and for being an influential impact to the community and the world. I also received an Executive Citation from Anne Arundel County Executive Steven R. Schuh recognizing my authenticity, passion, dedication and leadership in changing the way of others. And I also received the Prince Georges County Governor's Citation recognizing my contributions and influential impact on the community. I also received the Prince Georges County Executive Certificate of Recognition for commitment to serving and enriching communities and the world. THANK YOU VERY MUCH, DR. TASHEKA GREEN and your awesome team! What an honor to be recognized by your organization! I am grateful to have been chosen to be honored for serving, empowering and uplifting others. It brings tremendous fulfillment. I am reminded that Motel 6 had a motto that said, "We'll leave the light on for you." However, as I continue to travel along life's highway, endeavoring to fulfill the call on my life, I will do better than that: I will come alongside clients, weary travelers, those lost along life's journey, and those in need, to comfort them while in their holding pattern; and with God's help I will ensure that they arrive safely at their destination called purpose. It is my honor to serve God's precious people in a spirit of excellence. TO GOD BE ALL THE GLORY!

He said to them,

"Go into all the world

and preach the gospel

to all creation."

(Mark 16:15, NIV)

Michelle Boulden Hammond is a 48-year old multitalented woman that handles her faith, marriage, business and professional relationships with the power of inspiration. A small-town country girl from Talbot County, MD who has risen above life challenges from a birth defect to low self-esteem, rejection and mental abuse.

She received her Masters of Arts in Human Services in Counseling from Liberty University and holds CLC Certificate from International Coaching Federation. Michelle with her charismatic personality has the power that gives individuals influence to move beyond their now. In her book called Seize the Moment A Moment to Inspire which was released October 2017, she takes individuals on a 30-day affirmation and meditation journey that is life changing, Michelle is a member of the BSN Black Speakers Network and in this capacity, she has hosted and traveled nationally and internationally for women's empowerment conferences. In October 2018 she launched a group called TEAM M. A. B. B. (Mind, Affirmations,

Beauty & Boldness). This group featured 4 amazing ladies along with Michelle from the arenas of fashion, beauty and mental wellness. Michelle hosted Warm Your Heart, Warm Your Mind, Warm Your Soul, which is a spiritual awakening women's empowerment retreat for mind, body and soul and will be celebrating its 10th year.

Testimonial "My first time at #WHWMWS Michelle's retreat ... I discovered who I really Am... Her motivational talk session called My Life Evaluator was great. ~Judith~

On Facebook Live Social Media, she has now opened her platform of IAM2Inspire TV which features weekly at 7pm on Tuesdays.

Give Excellence A Standing Ovation

MICHELLE HAMMOND

As the writer of this story I want you as the reader to understand that you have not stumbled upon this book to read as a coincidence. It was a God-given appointment that you have been assigned to have this book. My desire as one of the co-authors of this chapter is that you affirm that you are designed with greatness. Throughout the days of your existence you shall have excellent character, wisdom and strength that will transform wherever you go. In the realm of character, the word of God states in the scripture reference Romans 5:3-5, NIV "Not only so, but we also glory in our sufferings, because we know that suffering produces perseverance; perseverance, character; and character, hope. And hope does not put us to shame, because God's love has been poured out into our hearts through the Holy Spirit, who has been given to us." So what is the importance of character? When we discuss character, we typically are describing the elements of the person's moral attributes. So as you begin to read some of my past, present and future about how I grew in developing character through my story to follow, it is my prayer that you be reminded that although tests and trials arise, never let your character down. However, it will take knowledge and wisdom which will build your strength when you are faced with opposition.

I will begin sharing a little bit of my life circumstances that have pruned me to become the woman I am today: a woman of excellence with notable character, wisdom and strength. Let's just say this road has not always been peaches and cream, but I am truly grateful for everything that has happened in my life. This is where I can take a break and declare it was acquiring the strength of endurance that has carried me thus far. I can recall moments when I believed that life was always going to be a struggle because of the obstacles I have faced within my life. I was born to a fifteen-year-old who herself struggled with a dysfunctional home life. In this not so stable setting, my biological grandmother decided that it would be best if I were given to a family that could better tend to my special needs. Yes, the special need was that I was born with a birth defect of my feet. However, I was not told I was adopted until I was 10 years of age. Upon learning this news, I always had in my mind that my mother just didn't want me. After all, the only thing I did know was that my adoptive mother was my real mother during this time. For years growing up, I always felt that I had identity issues of discovering just who I was after learning this news about my life. I continued to struggle with the feeling of rejection although my adoptive parents gave me all the essential acts of love and care I needed, but still I felt empty to really discovering who I really was.

When I was about nineteen years old my adoptive mother Betty and I had a heart-to-heart conversation about my life for the future. In this conversation she shared that she wanted me to connect with my biological mother and build a relationship with her. I felt confused and thought to myself, *why in the world would she want me to connect with someone who gave me away?* Well, in three weeks I understood why she asked me to do so. It was because three weeks later I encountered the most tragic loss of my life:

My adoptive mother died of diabetic complications that left her in a comatose state. I guess you can say that she was preparing me. My father and I had to make the decision whether to pull her off life support. When I tell you, I needed strength in this decision, I think I prayed literally for ten hours or more. I told my father we could not take her off this machine because I knew that God was going to bring her back. Unfortunately, the doctors advised us there were no signs of brain activity and that the life support machine was doing the breathing for her. I began at that moment becoming very angry and disappointed that God had taken the only mother that ever loved me and wanted me to become that confident woman she had always told me I would be. I will tell you that I solely relied on my mother for everything. You can say that my parents spoiled me. I wanted to go to college but at the time my parents couldn't afford to send me. So instead they told me if I worked, I wouldn't have to worry about transportation; they bought me my first car. In my mind this was the best option of a fair trade, but unfortunately this option changed because I had to work full time to help my father in the household. I had to jump into the responsibilities of womanhood quick. However, I really wanted to go to college.

A few months went by and my biological mother reached out to me tell me that she had adopted a little girl and she wanted me to come and meet her. I thought to myself, *how dare she ask me to come meet someone she adopted when she had given me away?* Initially this meeting was very awkward to me. In my mind I was talking to a total stranger that I knew nothing about, but why did she want to get to know me now? I left the meeting feeling as confused as I was in the beginning. Occasionally I would receive calls from her in which I thought maybe this could be the start of something called a mother/daughter relationship. It had been maybe three years after the death of my adoptive mother and now my biological mother apparently wanted to connect with me. I began opening my heart to her bit by bit, but still I could never ask the question: Why did you give me away? Years went by; I became pregnant with my first child and of course, who do you turn to for help when you need some clarity on how to raise a child? I thought your mother, but in my case, I felt I had no one to turn to. The reason is that I had asked her for help and her reply was not something I wanted to hear.

Initially during this time, I was a single mother struggling with homelessness. You as the reader may be asking yourself, *how did she become homeless when she was living with her dad?* Well unfortunately, I had never grieved, and my emotional stability was chaotic. As a result, I had made some decisions that were not the best choices. I left my father's home thinking I had found the love of my life, and this was disastrous as well. So I had to leave this abusive relationship thinking I could go to my mother for help and of course, she declined. Her response was "you made your bed so lie in it." In that moment I realized that once again I had to take the bitter with sweet. I also declared that I would never be placed in a position to ask her for anything. I will say that I began distancing myself from her, although she still would continue to call me to tell me each time she took on more adoptive children. At this time, she has now adopted four children. I can tell you that I was homeless for around two weeks. I did work and had some family members watch my son during this time. I felt embarrassment, shame and guilt but I hid this all with a smile. The walk of life just seemed to be crumbling down and the road was getting longer and longer to walk.

A social worker heard my cry and placed me and my son in a housing program. I then decided to go into long term care and began a career as a nursing assistant. My life seemed to have taken a turn for the better. However, working as a geriatric nursing assistant is very strenuous work. I felt that I needed more in my life. At this point in my life I had been working in this field for thirteen years and had another child and husband. I had to make a heartfelt decision to start my college career. So I enrolled in school and completed my Associate's Degree. My job where I worked as a geriatric nursing assistant promised that if I went to college, I would be receiving career advancement. The time had come for the job to deliver on their promise; however, they reneged on the deal. I was mad and disgusted. I thought to myself, *why does this keep happening to me?* In their response they said that I needed a bachelor's degree but at this time there would be no guarantee of job advancement. I remained hopeful and went to work with a smile, although I still had a bit of bitterness still inside.

So I enrolled into classes to get my Bachelor's Degree and received it eighteen months later. Well again, it seemed that life was going well. I then placed my resume for a position at the facility and was turned down again. They told me that I was not qualified and good enough to hold that position. I was crushed and believe me, this felt just like the moment when I had learned that I was adopted and that my mother didn't want me. One of the attributes I always have retained in my heart is hope. During this time, I had become involved in a church home that helped me deal with the things that I had struggled with in life, such as rejection, disappointment and forgiveness. So, in the reconciliation of not getting the job, I happened to be at a meeting and a job offer for community outreach became available.

I took the job after working at the nursing home for twenty-one years. My role as a community outreach worker stretched me out of my comfort zone and landed me in various atmospheres with public officials and state delegates. In this role I received numerous awards and the agency received multiple awards because of my work and the impact that I had introduced to the community. My presence and moral good character were just what the community needed, and I delivered it. Let me just mention sometimes we turn a blind eye when we lose focus and people will have you around for their benefit. I was about four years in this job and one day I was called to my director's office for a meeting, where he disclosed that I had 30 days and my job would end because they no longer needed my services. I saw stars and I was so shocked I could not move, but I wanted to slap the director through the wall. How could this happen? I was about to go to underwriting for my new home in two weeks. Well, I lost health insurance, the new home deal and business deals that I had gotten because of my affiliation with the job. However, I didn't lose my character and strength.

I was out of work for about three months and believe me, the struggle was real. In this three-month period, I was cleaning one day, and I stumbled across a journal that I had always written my feelings and expressions in. Well again, I will say that God brings things in your sight for a reason. I turned this journal into a book called *Seize A Moment to Inspire* and it was released in October 2017. The journey has been unbelievable ever since as a woman of excellence.

This is just a taste of some of the challenges that I faced, and I would like you as the reader to see that these conditions were my way of processing and demonstrating character. In all these circumstances I could have quit but I didn't. I know that God's plan is much better than my plan.

Basically, in the result of my relationship with my biological mother I will admit I still had bitterness toward her, but I did let forgiveness and love prevail. It wasn't the greatest, but I did respect her because she was my mother. So grab your seat. Remember I told you that I would never ask her for anything else pertaining to my life; however, she asked me a question. The question was if she died, would I take care of the youngest adoptees she was raising. The reason she asked was that she was diagnosed with stage four pancreatic cancer and only had a few months to live. My response was no, I will not take on this responsibility, because I had my own children to raise. I will say that this took a lot of courage and strength to tell someone who was worried about the welfare of her grandkids. I remembered my community resources, and they all were taken care of before she died on December 24, 2010. Prior to her dying she had assured me that she had life insurance, but when it was time to call in the benefit, I found out that the policy was invalid. I had to pay for the entire funeral. I had no help from any of the adopted children she raised. Yes, the child she had given away had to plan the funeral and provide her final resting place.

As for my adoptive father, my children and my husband decided it would be best that I move back to the house because my father was having health issues. Those skills that I had mastered as a geriatric nursing assistant helped me, especially when he fell ill suddenly and I had to take care of him. Instantly I thought about what would have happened if I had become disgruntled about them not giving me a job promotion. This surely would have messed up my assignment with him for the future. My daddy made me promise him that I wouldn't put him in a facility, and I did not. I worked long days and at night I took care of him. He died at the age of 92, living the best quality of life he could with the help of his daughter—me.

I distinctly learned through all the lessons in my life. Some were things that I could not control but God knew when these cases would arise. Although I must admit it has been challenging at times to remain positive in some of these circumstances, I could have been bitter and angry but instead I chose to become a woman of excellence. In my definition to the standards of my excellence I give a standing ovation. It is the result of not only being capable of rolling with the punches, but how you can take a swing. You cannot control everything that happens, but it is how you react to the outcome.

So being groomed with gaining character, wisdom, courage and strength has given me many awards. Today I am an entrepreneur, author and a history-maker as Talbot County, MD's first African American woman who has opened her own wellness center. The journey has only begun, and I'm ready to walk this runway as a Woman Walking in Virtue of Excellence with my crown of character, wisdom and strength.

A prayer for the reader:

Dear Heavenly Father, plant me in the path that you allow me to go while walking in this journey of virtue. May I have your devout favor of wise counsel set before me as I seek your face daily for strength, and structural foundation of character when opposition arrives. I thank you, My Jehovah God, for all your marvelous works of helping me become that outstanding role model of a person walking in excellence and giving you a standing ovation for your generosity in my life.

Lakita (Kita) Stewart-Thompson is a servant of the Lord, visionary, mother, mentor, entrepreneur, community and social advocate, philanthropist, teacher, bestselling-publisher and #1 best-selling author. She is the Founder/President of the National Association of Mothers & Daughters United Worldwide, Inc., which fosters "Better Bonds Between Daughters and Moms". Lakita is an award-winning community service advocate, winning the 2018 Achi Magazine DMV Woman of Influence Award, the 2018 Achi Magazine Servant Leader of the Year Award, the 2015 SheRose Unsung Organization Award and the 2016 Sisters-In-Law Pillars of Strength Award for her dedication and commitment to making a difference in the lives of women in the community.

Her ultimate desire is to have an international one stop resource center for women and girls seeking to overcome life altering traumatic circumstances through passion, purpose, partnerships, and philanthropy. Ms. Thompson resides in Maryland with her amazing daughter Destinee, the sunshine of her life! In her spare time, she enjoys quality time with her daughter, traveling, laughing, exploring new ventures, being creative, and hanging out with friends and family.

Cracked but Called

LAKITA STEWART-THOMPSON

Remembering a time when a darkness rested embedded in my
soul,
Where lightness could not illuminate,
Where my words refused to communicate.
This deep hurt, this deep pain subsisted to take my very breath
away.
It strangled me, took my life viciously;
It held me bound by some deep-seated inner realities.
It held me hostage against my will.
Emotionless, I sat still,
My heart incapacitated, unable to feel.
Simply the walking dead,
I was like cracked glass in a cupboard,
Once shattered into pieces
But simply glued back together again with facades, broken prom-
ises, misunderstandings and lies.
Broken on every side was I,
Misunderstood
And never the same,
Rejected, violated and being constantly called out of my name,
Just simply placed in a box where filthy hands often came.
But in that cupboard, I remained,

All cracked up but still being used,
Visibly exposed but quietly in pain,
Internally drenched with ice cubes of shame,
Overwhelmingly divulged with blame though cleansed often in
   what felt like flames—
Flames that overcame my mind.
Contaminated on the inside,
So Broken and fragile was I—
Not made in China but I wore that disguise,
Being filled with contents that my creator denies.
Sitting in the cupboard all I could do is cry;
As long as I sat there, I believed every last lie:
That I was cracked and shattered to pieces, broken, and unable to
   be fixed.
So I lost my identity in the mix,
Abused and abandoned,
Every crack and every crevice exposed me, damaged me emotionally.
I wonder if the other broken glasses in the cupboard would speak.
I want to know if when they are filled do they too leak?
Do they too feel weak and seek to be thrown to the floor?
Did they feel less useful and not to be drunk from anymore?
Suicidal and worthless,
As I sat in the cupboard, I remember being picked up by unknown
   hands; I remember never waiting to be used again.
I am simply cracked sitting in this cupboard of life,
But I had to identify my self-worth,
So when I began reflecting on my shattered pieces
I discovered that yes, I have cracks and I have crevices
And yes, I may leak at times
But I am a vessel that can be used despite my abnormalities.
I am a child of the most High.
I am Cracked but called.

Today, I stand as an imperfect woman who has survived rejection, self-mutilation, molestation, bullying, attempted suicide, being held at gunpoint, multiple accidents where each car was totaled, rejection, divorce, and the list goes on.

At a very young age, I tried my first drink of alcohol, had my first unwanted sexual encounter, and experienced a gun to my head. I also recall the feeling of rejection from people who should have loved me but neglected and took advantage me, from those who mistreated me every chance they could but used the words "I love you." I used razor blades often to ease my pain. When that didn't work, I took all the pills I could out of the medicine cabinet and as I was fighting to live during what felt like my darkest hour, a family member whispered in my ear, "You didn't try hard enough." This left a wound so deep within my soul that I remained in pain for years thereafter and continued making attempts to leave this world. This moment defined me and followed me throughout my life. I found myself fighting to live often, leaving me to seek approval from others even if it hurt. I believed I deserved it. I carried depression in and out of relationships. It took a failed marriage for me to deal with some suppressed realities about myself and my haunting past. Though I've experienced greater pain, this particular failure hurt me the most. It uncovered every one of my insecurities. My wounds paralyzed me and went unresolved for years. I did not know who I was. I lost my identity and became what others wanted me to be. The unseen scars on my heart were very destructive in every relationship I encountered. I created invisible walls to block anyone from gaining access. I wore an armored disguise daily to give the perception that I was strong and had it all together. However, my soul was lost, broken, low, battered, lonely, beaten, and confused.

As a result of the trauma I experienced, I lived with depression for many, many years with no idea, nor did I know God. I knew of God but not personally. The hardest thing I have ever had to do in life is forgive and love myself. I blamed myself and allowed every circumstance to define me and my self-worth. Today I stand, cracked but called, knowing that I was called according to His purpose.

Romans 8:28, KJV "And we know that all things work together for good to them that love God, to them who are the called according to his purpose."

My story is simple; I am Cracked but called! Called to love, called to serve, called to share, and called to give.

My cracks were preparing me for the call of purpose God has placed upon my life. I live each day to share with the world that I am a living, breathing testimony. Despite it all, I am still here. I have learned that with God ALL things are possible to those who believe. We all have had things in our life try to destroy us but God created us to endure what seems like the hardest things in life to prepare us for such a time as this. I found that it was all necessary. Our life challenges are never to break us but ultimately to make us. Adversity is a tool that prepares us for the calling that God has pre-ordained for us to walk in. This chapter is to give you hope from my painful journey to my purposed journey. It is to encourage you and let you know no matter what, everything is going to be all right. Trouble will come but it will not remain.

In 2008 I gave birth to a little bubbly girl, and this changed my life completely. God began to speak to me in ways I have never heard. He gave me a vision to change lives through my words.

At the time there was a lot of chaos in my life. I simply wasn't in a position to help change anyone's life, let alone write anything. Though I would journal and write poetry throughout my life to release my pain, I never had any intentions of sharing it with anyone. Writing was never a passion, but simply an outlet. It was my therapy. I always wondered why I ever existed. I felt like an outcast all my life and truly believed my life was meaningless. Yes, God existed, I knew that, but I really couldn't seem to find him in my mess of a life.

Something happened inside of me after I had a paralysis moment (encounter with God). I began seeking counsel. It was during counseling that I was prompted to revisit my failed marriage. I also was challenged to examine some roots that were planted before marriage. I found that I was skipping through life by burying everything inside. I hid behind multiple jobs at a time, classes, church activities, busyness, relationships and helping everybody else.

As a result of allowing God to work in me, I realized my purpose. Your pain was specifically designed to bring out the purpose in you. My purpose has become my passion. That passion is writing and helping others to express themselves through writing. God gave me a platform to assist women to find healing and hope through their very own words, while helping others do the same. It will inspire many to lean on God as a source of healing, deliverance, and restoration. It is also to serve women and girls who have experienced trauma; therefore, I created a non-profit.

No matter what you've gone through or are even now going through, God is able. No matter how much you think you are not important, God loves you. There is hope! You have a purpose! The very tests you endure will determine that purpose. So whatever area in life you are being challenged in, understand that He is preparing you for your next steps in life.

We all have experienced hurt at some point in our lives. It could have been mental, physical, emotional, or spiritual, etc. As we go about life living with our silent pain, we either will experience the pain of change or we will experience the pain of staying the same. Most of us stay the same and never address our innermost hurts. Throughout life I've heard many say, "Hurt people, hurt people." So we end up hurting one another as a result of our very own issues, which leads to dysfunction in our homes, marriages, children, jobs, relationships, and the list goes on. "He heals the brokenhearted and binds up their wounds [curing their pains and sorrows]" (Psalm 147:3, NIV).

To all in battle, fighting against one of life's many struggles, you're not alone. Prayerfully you begin to unlock the doors of peace, healing, and restoration as you read through these pages. Don't give up; you have so much to live for, and remember your pain has a purpose.

"And we know that in all things God works for the good of those who love him, who have been called according to his purpose."

(Romans 8:28, NIV)

As a woman who endured 18 years of infertility, Tameka Chapman knows what it means to persevere through some of life's toughest situations. Having feelings of loneliness and not seeing her own self-worth and self-value, she isolated herself from family and friends and chose to suffer alone. After years of sadness, shame, and tears, she knew things had to change. She successfully crafted her own path to living a successful life, including the birth of her two children, and now offers women the same opportunity to living their greatest life.

As the Founder/CEO of Women Persevering for Greatness, a women's empowerment platform that specializes in showing women how to make daily changes in their lives in order to reach their greatest potential, she helps women overcome self-doubt, fears and limiting beliefs that keep them stuck and stagnate. Women walk away fully equipped, educated and empowered to actively pursue their dreams.

When she is not inspiring other women, Tameka loves spending time with Deone, her husband of 20 years, and two children, Aspen and Arden. She also loves singing, sewing, reading, laughing, and road trips.

In Pursuit of My Faith

TAMEKA CHAPMAN

I've always lived my life as a life of faith and everything about me, including the battles that I've endured, resonates with Matthew 17:20, If you can have faith the size of a mustard seed, anything is possible. Faith has been poured into me since I was a little girl. I have several women in my life who showed me how to be prayerful and truly believe that when I pray and ask God for something, He will provide, no matter how long it takes. Because of the many challenges that I've faced in my life, I know without a doubt that God is in the blessing business. And my life is a true testament of His abundant outpouring of gifts and I must continue to be a blessing to others with the gifts that God has blessed me to have.

It was the early part of summer in 2001; I was a young woman and a newlywed. My husband and I had been married since 1999 and were just starting to live life and make family plans. We made plans for a true vacation and had planned to visit several beaches, historical places and monuments. The countdown had begun, and we only had two weeks before our EPIC vacation was to begin. We were in the initial stages of trying to start our own family and wanted to get a good trip in before we would have to settle down for a while. While wrapping up final details, I had a doctor's appointment and that appointment not only cancelled our EPIC vacation, but instantly changed our lives.

At this doctor's appointment, I was told that I needed to be immediately admitted to the hospital because my blood levels were so low that the doctors were unsure how I was still able to do all that I was doing, which included running a very successful in-home childcare program with five toddlers. I even overheard one doctor state that he didn't understand how I was still alive. Needless to say, I became very concerned because I've never heard a doctor question my existence. I was overrun with emotions and questions and no one seemed to have the answers.

Why wasn't this caught before now? I'd had bloodwork done in the recent past, so why didn't they say something then? What happened now? I was told that I needed to have a blood transfusion right away if I was to survive. They were acting as if I'd been wheeled in on a stretcher and was bleeding from every crevice of my body. All I could think was, *where is my husband? Why isn't he already here to bring some calmness to me, my soul and this beige room?* As soon as I began to think of him, he entered the room with a smile on his face, reassuring me that he was there to watch everything that was happening. God was listening to me ask for my needs.

As the hours passed, I remembered that I started talking to God and asking Him to spare my life because I knew I had more work to do in this world. I promised Him then that when He spared my life, I would forever speak of His greatness, mercy and favor to all who would listen. Once I spoke it, I knew that He heard my cry and would prolong my life not just for me, but because there were a number of people that needed to see me exhibit my faith level and not waver because it wasn't the cool thing to do. As a young lady and newly married, it was a lot to think about and there were many more questions that ran through my mind. How did my husband feel that his new wife was facing a life-threatening medical issue? Would he still view me as his better half? Would he still love me as he said he did?

These were all thoughts that the devil was using to make me doubt everything that I knew about faith, my marriage and my love for God.

The doctors entered the room and started advising us of the procedure, the risks (which included the risk of my body rejecting the blood and causing more issues) and gave me many forms to read and sign. I was so overwhelmed and didn't know what to do except talk to God. I asked Him to allow the right doctors to be in the room and to touch the hearts and hands of each person involved. All that I could rely on was my faith and knowing that my husband would never leave my side. After a two-day hospital stay, we were released with instructions to follow up in a week. I stayed in constant prayer as I continued to ask God to help me increase my faith that would surpass all understanding.

For the next 12 months, I was fine and didn't worry about what had happened. Or so I thought. In the fall of 2002, we were once again having to deal with my depleted blood levels. I had lost so much blood this time that the doctors felt it necessary to call for the chaplain to provide some soul comfort. I was immediately admitted again with the same procedure explained and was seen by the same doctors as the year before. This time, even when caught off-guard again, I was better equipped and prepared because I was prayed up and in tune with my soul and faith. They say if you stay ready, you don't have to get ready. So I practiced keeping my faith level on full for times like this. For the doctors to have the chaplain visit was great because I had someone to pray with me, not over me. I may have looked like death was knocking at my door, but God said NO again.

I felt that God was taking me through this battle because a lesson needed to be learned and His devotion to me because of my faith in Him needed to be on full display. Even when times got rough and I wasn't feeling well, I never questioned why. Many people didn't understand my calm demeanor and smile, but I had a secret power that many are afraid to tap into and use. I had unshakeable faith!

Trying to find a new normal after having a second blood transfusion was a bit frustrating because of the number of doctor visits and the number of blood tests that had to be run. The doctors didn't know how to prevent me from having to go through this again, and that only fueled me to pray more, pray harder and truly believe that God has me, no matter what! Year after year for the next four years we had no incidents, allowing us and the doctors to become a bit more relaxed in my monthly visits. By 2005, I was only seeing the doctors twice a year.

In the spring of 2006, we had to face another blood transfusion. The doctors began to question me about what had happened in the six months since my last appointment. This time, I felt a shift in the room. I felt something was a bit different in the way the doctors talked. I never experienced doctors freely showing belief. The doctors had started to believe that once again my life would be spared and that I would overcome another transfusion. I attributed their now-calm stance to the faith that I continued to show in my walk and talk. I remember making a joke with them that the third time's the charm. I advised them they'd now learned their lesson and I no longer had to be the vessel for them. As we proceeded with the third blood transfusion, they advised me that my body would eventually stop accepting the transfusions after having too many. I responded, "This is the last time and I'll be fine."

As I learned more about my faith and became more comfortable with showing my faith, my life became better and easier. I remembered my promise to God in 2001 and that gave me immediate peace in knowing that He keeps His promises and I would make sure to keep my promise to Him. It has now been 13 years and I haven't ever had to revisit this type of trauma and grief again. I'm grateful that I allowed myself to remember my teachings as a child and have that crazy faith that what I believed could and would happen.

I now encourage each of you to let go of the pressures from society to not walk in your faith. In today's world, when many are not being true stewards of God's word, and many refuse to give God credit for where they are in life and the many blessings that they've received in life, be the one to stand out! Stand out while standing in your faith and watch how God starts and continues to abundantly bless your life.

Dr. Theresa A. Moseley is originally from North Carolina. She is a US Army veteran, member of the Screen Actors Guild, and life member of the National Association for Black School Educators (NABSE). Dr. Moseley attended Georgia State University, Bowie State University and The American University where she graduated in 1988 with a PHD. In 2014, she published her first novel, The Fourth Child Five Decades of Hope. Dr. Moseley is a motivational speaker, humanitarian and world traveler who has lived in Germany and Turkey. She also traveled to Great Britain, Italy, France, Spain, Australia, New Zealand, Hawaii, Brazil, Morocco, Mexico, and Canada.

Dr. Moseley has been in the field of education for 24 years. In 1999, Dr. Moseley was awarded the Excellence in Education Award from the Prince George's County Chamber of Commerce. In 2006, she was recognized as Prince George's County Outstanding Educator. In 2013, Dr. Moseley was awarded the Excellence in Gifted and Talented Education Award from the Maryland Department of Education.

She currently has a campaign for Creating Ambassadors of Peace: No More Violence, One School, One Community, One County at a time. Dr. Moseley's future goals are to establish a foundation to support world peace. She believes everyone should be an Ambassador for Peace.

Creating Ambassadors of Peace

DR. THERESA A. MOSELEY

Living in a world that is filled with love, peace, and joy may sound surreal to some. Some think it's an unrealistic goal to have, as there will always be people who hate others for whatever reason. Some believe there will always be violence in the world somewhere. I remember when the terrorists attacked on 9/11, this country came together—black, white, Democrat, Republican, rich and poor. Congress stood together, united, on the steps of the capital. Nations reached out to support us. People were kind to one another. I prayed that the harmony would last, but it was short-lived. A year later in 2002 when the sniper murders occurred, our citizens in the Washington Metropolitan Area were in fear. People were afraid to put gas in their car. Everyone stayed clear of white vans. Once again, people came together to support the victims and looked after one another. That was also short-lived. These two incidents impacted the world but they impacted me personally. My brother lived in New York City and would have been on the PATH train to Jersey that morning, but he didn't go for some reason. My daughter was a student at Benjamin Tasker Middle School when the sniper shot a student just 15 minutes after my daughter's bus arrived. Fortunately, she was okay, but a young student was shot. My mind began to wonder about these incidents. What if my brother had taken that train in New York? What if my daughter's bus had arrived 15 minutes earlier? Incidents of violence in the world impact everyone in some way, shape or form. It makes you think about what you can do to make a difference. It makes me want to make the world a more peaceful place.

I wondered what makes a person violent. Surely, they don't come out of the womb that way. After reading several books and reviewing some old theories and practices I learned in graduate school, I came to realize that the psychosocial development of the child does impact whether he or she will be a healthy person. I realized that parents, teachers, community, and society play a role in that development. If we could make sure that our children gain all the virtues they need in each stage of life, we may be able to make this nation a more peaceful place to live.

I remember being in Sunday School and reading scriptures on peace: "Blessed are the peacemakers for they shall be called the children of God" (Matthew 5:9, KJV). I thought of Mother Teresa of Calcutta, Mahatma Gandhi, and Martin Luther King as peacemakers as I read about their values and beliefs in our society. I never thought of my responsibility as a peacemaker until December of 2007 at the National Society of High School Scholars. I heard a speech by Claes Nobel, grandnephew of Alfred Nobel. During his speech, he told the students they all had academic excellence. "Now go into the world and become Ambassadors of Peace."

As an educator, I was excited to spread this message to my students. When I went back to work, I immediately began to think, *what can I do help create Ambassadors of Peace?* I asked God to guide me in the direction to help me discover my divine purpose. Deep inside, I knew my purpose was about helping others and teaching people to love. I just did not know which direction I needed to take to fulfill that purpose. One night I was dreaming about a song I sang in high school. It was the prayer of St Francis.

"Lord, make me an instrument of Your peace. Where there is hatred, let me sow love; where there is injury, pardon; where there is doubt, faith; where there is despair, hope; where there is darkness, light; where there is sadness, joy." This was my favorite song to sing with the choir. I've always thought about what the world would be like if the world was at peace. After dreaming about this song, I made it the framework for creating Ambassadors of Peace. I was in a position where I could help children who had no faith, self-doubt, despair, and no hope by bringing light into their lives and helping them discover that they have a divine purpose on earth. No matter what is going on in their lives, there is a light inside of them that shines so brightly. That light will bring them peace and harmony.

One night after reading Matthew 5:15-16, I discovered what I had to do. "Ye are the light of the world. Let your light shine before men, that they may see your good works." I was living in my purpose; however, I had a charge to teach others to live in theirs. I started to think about all the conventional wisdom and funded knowledge I achieved over the years and decided to be intentional in creating Ambassadors of Peace. One person can make a difference in the world. If everybody took ownership of the effort toward peace, there would be no despair. If everyone discovered their divine purpose, we all could be spreading love, peace, and joy.

I used to teach my graduate students the importance of understanding the psychosocial development of students. Most of my graduate students were classroom teachers. Erik Erikson developed eight stages of psychosocial development and emphasized culture and society have an impact on personality, which is developing over life. The parents and the caregivers have the most important role during the first two stages, where the child learns trust vs. mistrust and autonomy vs. shame and doubt. The child will either learn the virtues of hope and will or negative outcomes of fear and shame. The classroom teacher has a major role in stage 4 of the child's life. They are in school and learning how to be competent. If the student does not have the opportunity to be industrious and learn the virtue of competence, then he or she will feel inferior. When that happens, these children will struggle during their school years and life.

Dr. Ken Magid and Carole A. McKelvy wrote a book called *High Risk Children Without a Conscience*. Their findings are consistent with Erikson. "What happens, right or wrong, in the critical first two years of a baby's life will imprint that child as an adult." Although we don't get the students until the fourth and fifth stage of development, we need to recognize that we have some students who never learned to trust and don't have the will or purpose because they did not develop these virtues during the first three stages of life. The outcome is fear, suspicion, shame, and inadequacy. Finally, they are in your classroom where they must learn the virtue of competence. It's very difficult to be competent when you don't have hope, will, and purpose.

The teacher plays a major role in this development; however, if you don't answer all the questions, recognize the deficiencies, give everyone a response opportunity, communicate with parents and give the child hope, the student will feel inferior.

God gave me the gift of intuition and I can always determine which students are missing the virtues that lead to competence. It takes time, but if you listen to the student to determine what they are feeling and how they think, you can help them change some behaviors. If we don't address the students who need our attention, especially those without a conscience, they may end up in prison or dead at a young age. On the other hand, they may be responsible for the death of another child who will not able to live their divine purpose because their life was cut short by someone without a conscience.

I realized that there was a connection between the psychosocial development of people and violent crimes in our world. There is a lot of research out on serial killers being unattached children. If we could assist the families with small children who are troubled because they lack trust and will, if we could address those students in class who are not competent and lack purpose, if we could have a systemic approach to developing healthy students starting in nursery school, I believe we could educate productive law-abiding citizens and peacemakers.

As an administrator, I attend several International Baccalaureate (IB) trainings. IB is an international education foundation head-quartered in Geneva, Switzerland which offers four programs. My high school offered the IB Diploma Program. The program has extensive training. I would use strategies I learned during IB professional development with my students. One day I had over 300 students in the auditorium. I posted pictures of troubling violent events in the world on the overhead. I asked them to tell me what they saw, how they thought about what they saw, and how it made them feel. Next, I asked them, "How does the event impact the world? How does it impact your community, and how does it impact you?" Finally, the students were ready for a real discussion on violence in the world and how it impacts them, even when it's not in their community. It was amazing how a class of 300-plus were attentive and had strong opinions about the violence in the world. My final thought: "You can make a difference. Become an Ambassador of Peace. Communicate, don't retaliate. Listen with your eyes and ears. See something, say something. Have a peaceful conversation with your peers and don't believe all you see on social media."

Some schools have a large number of repeat offenders. The same students are suspended all the time. When this happens, it's obvious just giving a consequence is not working. I would ask, "What was the activating event? How did it make you feel? What did you do?" This is the first thing to do as opposed to yelling out consequences for the behavior. That's a quick way to get the student more upset. What's really disturbing is sometimes students fight over the most trivial things. "He looked at me wrong. I heard he was talking about me." You must get the students to understand the irrational behaviors and change them to more appropriate behaviors. After a consequence is given for the behavior, you must follow up and follow through on anything you promised. It's our responsibility to help them find that light inside them. If one is filled with hate and anger, there is a dark presence. We have to rid them of that darkness and help them find the light inside them that will lead to their divine purpose and help them to be productive and peaceful citizens.

One day while I was monitoring the halls during lunch, I ran into a student who was clearly not where he was supposed to be. When I saw, him I asked, "Hi son! Where are you supposed to be?" "Art class." "Okay. So why are you in the hall?" The student smiled. His face lit up like a bright star. When I saw his smile, I said, "Oh my goodness, what a beautiful smile. What do you want to do with your life?" "I play football!" "Are you good?" "Yes, ma'am!" "That's what's up! Do you want to go to college and play football?" "Yes, ma'am!" "Then you need to go to class every day. Stay out of the halls. Ask questions when you don't understand something. You need to have a decent SAT score and grade point average. All the time you spend practicing football, you need to spend twice the time studying." He smiled again. We talked for about 15 minutes. As he was about to go to class I said, "Hey, pull your pants up!" The student smiled and said, "Yes ma'am!" "By the way, if you ever want to model, I know an agent you can share with your mom." He smiled and began to walk down the hall. As he turned the corner, he looked back at me. As he turned right to go down another hall, a small tear rolled down my cheek. Two weeks later he was dead.

I attended my cousin's wedding in Punta Cana in December of 2013. On the flight back, I received a text message when my plane landed. The message said I had a missing student. A few hours later it was confirmed that he was shot to death. I immediately recalled the meeting I had with him in the hallway. We talked for 15 minutes. Little did I know that those 15 minutes were important, as I was asked to speak at his funeral. I was very sad and upset that someone would take the life of another. Every day I think about this student. It took a while for my students to calm down, as their friend was well-liked by his peers. I wondered who did this, but I also wondered what I could do to create peace for my students. I thanked God for giving me the wisdom to talk to this young man in the hall that day. Everything happens for a reason.

The next school year, I had another student murdered. He was beaten to death in a park. I attended his wake and watched all of his friends mourn. That night when I was reading my Bible, I came across this scripture: "Blessed are they that mourn: for they shall be comforted" (Matthew 5:4, KJV). The next day I decided to create an eight-foot banner for this student. I knew this would provide comfort for his friends. He was an artist so I knew his mother would appreciate the symbolic gesture for her son. The students drew a sunrise and sunset and wrote notes to him on the banner. They called him the Golden Boy. As a result, I purchased a bouquet of gold and white balloons. I called all of his friends to the front lawn of the school and had a trumpet player perform. The students held the banner as I released the balloons. As soon as the balloons floated in the air, it began to snow. There was no snow in the forecast. I believe it was the spirit of my deceased student, letting us know he was pleased and that he was at peace. The students went back to class and finally felt a sense of peace. I facilitated several small group meetings with these students to follow up on their feelings and to see how they were doing. Follow-up is very important in every aspect. I prayed to God for me not to lose any more students to violence. I've lost students before to car accidents, heart disease, and other illnesses. Losing a student to violence is heartbreaking. They had their whole life ahead of them and they will not live out their divine purpose. Facing the death of my students to violent crimes, I never lost faith in my God and had the strength and wisdom to reach out to my communities and speak publicly about making the world a peaceful place.

During the summer, while on vacation, I decided to have a full campaign for No More Violence – One City, One State, One Nation at a Time. I purchased shirts for teachers and students. I told the students if they wore the shirts, they could wear jeans. Every Friday, we wore the shirts to promote No More Violence. We also had a 5K run for No More Violence in the spring, created by one of my students and her mother to support our effort for No More Violence.

A few months later, I was watching the news and I saw a familiar street. My cousins lived on that street. As I continued to watch the news, I realized it was my cousin who was murdered. She was shot to death in her home in Baltimore. She was a great woman who had Bible study in her home every Wednesday. Why would someone murder her? I always knew that there was a problem with gun violence in our nation. However, any violence is a problem. I was blessed not to have any more students murdered during my principalship; however, the violence in the nation and world continues. The number of school shootings continues to rise in our nation. As a result, the next school year the campaign to end violence was again No More Violence – One City, One State, One Nation at a Time.

When a student initiates a violent act in school and only receives a consequence with no treatment, there is a strong possibility he or she will be violent again and the antisocial behavior will continue. Be proactive, not reactive with these students. Its everyone's responsibility to create Ambassadors of Peace.

I use the theories of Albert Ellis and Erik Erikson on a regular basis to help parents, students, and teachers. I agree with Erikson that the personality is developed over time and the formative years are very important in creating healthy students. My job as a parent, educator, and humanitarian is to provide hope to all of those in need of love and support. Getting students to talk about how they feel as opposed to acting out how they feel is very important, as is getting parents to understand that we are partners and we want to help them grow and develop healthy children. It is the teacher's responsibility in the fourth stage of life to help the student develop the virtue of competence. Recognize those students that don't have hope and will and get them assistance. All educators should understand human growth and development and be able to recognize the missing links that are preventing a child from being a productive citizen. If we get them help, perhaps we can prevent antisocial behavior.

In order for the world to be a more peaceful place, we must be respectful to everyone, kind, caring, empathetic, active listeners, and Ambassadors of Peace. I am an Ambassador of Peace and diligent in creating others. I reflect on the song I sang in high school. I teach students where there is doubt, have faith. Where there is despair, have hope. Where there is darkness, bring light. Where there is sadness, bring joy. I learned from all of my experiences, both positive and negative. If a lesson was learned, then every experience is positive, thus sadness brings joy. There are no accidents in life. Everything, positive and negative, happens for a reason. Listen to your dreams. God speaks to us through dreams. God tells us what we need to do. When you have been given your purpose, you must act on it. Recognize that it's not about you but helping others. I encourage everyone to listen to your heart; search deep in your soul. Listen to God, and discover what your purpose is. Utilize that purpose to help others.

As I continue my journey as a Woman of Virtue Walking in Excellence, not only do I walk in excellence, but I demonstrate excellence through creating Ambassadors of Peace. Ambassadors of Peace is not just a saying; it is a movement that will change a community, neighborhood, and world. I charge every adult, parent, community, teacher, educator and student to think about what they can do to make this world a more peaceful place. It's important that our children see who we are as Women of Virtue Walking in Excellence. They can see the Character, Wisdom, Courage, and Strength through our resilience and ability to overcome obstacles that are a part of everyday life. In order to maintain these characteristics, we must have faith in our God, understand the process of living in our purpose, and believe in ourselves no matter what. Go to a quiet place and listen to your soul. Our choices and actions matter. Remember, life is but a short road to our ultimate destiny. Make peace, have compassion, and learn to love before you get there.

Sources

Erikson, Erik. (1950). *Childhood and Society*, W.W. Norton & Co.: New York, NY.

Magid, Ken & McKelvey, Carole. (1987). *High Risk Children Without a Conscience*. Bantam Books: New York, NY.

Holy Bible. (1979). King James Version. Holman Bible Publishers: Nashville, TN.

"Blessed are the

peacemakers, for they

will be called children

of God."

(Matthew 5:9, NIV)

TRIVIA PAYNE currently resides in Baltimore City, the city of her birth and upbringing. She is the founder and Executive Director of Bondage to Grace Connections, which was established in February 2017 as a nonprofit for children affected by incarceration. For the past 9 years, she has been the chief coordinator for the Grace Beyond the Walls Summer Camp.

Trivia has five daughters and a son, and finds joy in making sure that they are all working towards the gifts that God has instilled in them. She is also a mother in law and a grandmother to "Mr. Wonderful".

Trivia has received multiple parent volunteer awards, led several PTA organizations as president, and was the class mother for CIVITAS class of 2012. In 2009, Trivia married a childhood friend, Pastor Antoine Payne of Grace Beyond the Walls church. Together, they founded The Philemon Ministry, a mentoring community that supports men from incarceration into stable living.

Trusting God with My Virtue

TRIVIA PAYNE

Being charged with the task to write about "Women of Virtue - Walking in Excellence" has given me a reminder of just who God has called me to be. As I think about the journey that God has allowed me to travel, I wish I had read Proverbs 31 long before 2018, at least with the ounce of understanding that I have today. In the past, hearing this story about this workaholic woman gave me both excitement and reservation. The excitement is because I know that God has bestowed greatness in me and the reservation because of being a good woman.

Recently, I came to the realization that there is a relationship between power and virtue. It is when the opportunity was presented to me to write about myself and how I walk in virtue that enlightened my perspective about the importance of walking in my God-given authority. Reflecting on Proverbs 31 verses 10 through 31, I am reminded of how important my role is as a mother, as a wife, and as an entrepreneur. These roles are not only important to God, they are also important as to how I am to live according to the measure of faith that God has ordained for me to walk in.

There are many directions that I could have chosen to share my story to explain my walk, but where I will start is with my current position in God. This year there was a major shift in my family's life. It's not like as a family we hadn't overcome things, but for the first time in my life, I had to set my mind to the reality that I am really an adult. It didn't help that for a whole year, I was asked if I was ready to become an empty nester. When first asked, I was preparing to become a grandmother for the first time and in my mind my girls would go to school close to home, but at whatever rate, my husband would be with me.

That all changed. In 2018, my first granddaughter was stillborn, my middle daughter graduated high school and started attending Bowie State, I had challenges I was praying though, and writing my dissertation became daunting. Now to fast forward to this year, my oldest daughter and son–in–love, who lost their first child, delivered my first grandson (Mr. Wonderful), my last two daughters graduated from high school and are set to attend Frostburg State University, which is three hours away, and I have been struggling as to whether or not completing my dissertation is even an option. Now I found myself going back and forth, trying to decide which way I am going to go from here.

So let's go back just a bit. When I became pregnant at the young age of 17, life for me really didn't look too good. I couldn't have cared less about myself and my self-esteem was nonexistent. Once I had my daughter, I went through many challenging processes because I was pregnant and living at home with my mother alone. When I told my mother about the possibility of being pregnant, I remember thinking she was going to kill me, but I was going to have my baby. As I think about it, I believed this child would be someone who would love me. As years went by, living from place to place with this beautiful little girl, I ended up pregnant again. During the nine months of my pregnancy, there were several traumatic experiences, that could have caused me to give up on life if I had not been grounded in the character, wisdom, courage and strength of God.

My experiences were nothing short of the power of God. It was through God's anointing that I was able to overcome these traumatic experiences. I began to discover that my world had to have a purpose. I had to overcome the wiles of those who tried to stop me from achieving greatness. Life for me has been nothing short of interesting. There were many heartaches, disappointments, and failures, but I had to change my mindset and start to believe I am who God says I am. I started learning what was important to me. I decided to start making defined goals. The most important thing I had to learn was to walk in the power and virtue that was created in me.

There is not a day that goes by that I am not seeking God's movement in my life. For many years I lived my life in the shadows of others. If I was told that something was wrong with something that I had been doing, I would try my best to correct it. What I have recently discovered is that just because "others" believe that there is something wrong with you doesn't mean that "they" are correct. What I didn't realize was that every time I tried to correct the problem, I was causing more strife, not only with the other person, but with myself. I had to learn how to maintain my integrity, walk in character, and continue the ordered steps which God had ordained.

Even though I was maintaining my walk, there were still thoughts that I would never amount to anything, due to the nature of my environment. I prayed, trusted God, and activated my faith, and through it all, God moved in mighty ways. For most of my life, I lived under the thoughts of others, and thought I had to become what they wanted me to become, rather than becoming what God had created me to be. I was living to please others, rather than living to please God. However, I knew in the depths of my soul that God is real, and He had called me to become a success and to walk in greatness. God continued to show up in my life and make ways out of no way. I often refer to the movement of God in my life as a result of me having crazy faith. Therefore, when I am feeling the weight of the journey I am pursing, I continue to strive for better, knowing that God will never leave me nor forsake me.

God is moving in my life every day, every minute, every hour. He continues to prove His love toward me and show me how to walk in virtue and demonstrate excellence. This was made clear to me in 2015, when I sensed that God was leading me to begin my writing journey. I heard clear directions that made a lot of sense. The instructions to me were "you are going to write a book about your testimony." But the thoughts didn't stop there; I also remember hearing, "Your book won't be written until you have completely read a book." Being who I am, I thought that the process would be easy. I have purchased many books. The problem was that I had not read through an entire book in my adult life.

I thought I could do this task in one week. I started telling people what I thought God was saying. I started preparing the book in my mind. It wasn't uncommon for God to drop a notion in my head, and I would want to bring the world along with me. I began telling my friends and family to start writing in hopes that they would be on board to bring this vision to pass. What I missed was I didn't hear in the message that I would be taking anyone with me, so at the time, the vision for writing the book was halted.

This went on for three years. Life was happening before my eyes and I had yet to read a book. In 2016, I heard this voice again. But the difference at this time was that I had been sitting in a room full of people who were doing what I believed God had given me at the time. They were telling their stories and I was feeling bad because I knew that was the vision I had in 2015. It had been the first time that I was invited to intentionally give my testimony and knew that I was being shown "if God tells you to do something, you better do it." God has no problem using someone else.

Again, I heard that still voice saying, "Just read a book, any size. Just read. Once you have finished reading you will begin to write." I prayed as I always did and asked God what and how I would complete the task at hand. This time the prayer was a little different. I asked God to give me the wisdom and what I needed to accomplish the task at hand. I remembered buying a set of books that I shared with a group of pastors' wives that summer and the book was less than 150 pages. I had been reading the book since I bought it, but it seemed I was getting nowhere. In 2018, after continually having this thought, I prayed and within days, I had completed reading the book, by Naomi W. Carter. I enjoyed the book AND it revealed to me what I believed God was calling me to.

It wasn't until I read the entire book that what I had asked God for in prayer years before actually came to pass. In the early 2000s, after attending conference after conference, I decided that I wanted to be a motivational speaker. I wanted to be that woman who could impact the lives of many on a larger scale. When I finished reading that book in 2018, I heard that still voice again saying, "Now you can speak. You had to read in order to write and in order to speak you have to learn to write." It didn't come as a surprise at that time because I was at the height of writing my dissertation and my life was beginning to connect.

I began writing my first book, which I am still working on, in October of 2018 but I have completed two collaborative projects and I have written four articles. I have completed my unpublished personal story and have been invited to speak at several local events.

Currently, I am not only watching God move in my life, I am trusting God with the process and walking gracefully in the things that he has for me. Coming from a place where I was a young mother of five daughters, trying to find my way to overcoming obstacle after obstacle, God saw fit to allow me to watch all five of my girls graduate high school and me to become an entrepreneur while helping others do the same.

Walking in virtue does not mean that life is going to be all glory all the time. It does not even mean that the challenges won't come. Walking in virtue means that we are willing to take the curve balls and strive to make it to home base. The key is that one must accept his or her God-given authority and trust God with the outcome (virtue).

*"Trust in the LORD
with all your heart and
lean not on your own
understanding; in all your
ways submit to him,
and he will make your
paths straight."*

(Proverbs 3:5-6, NIV)

Kimberly Hobbs is an international bestselling author, as well as a faith life coach, and leader having a "heart's passion" to encourage and coach others to develop a more POWERFUL connective relationship with their creator. She has had interviews with Moody Bible Radio, "God at Work" and various television appearances, sharing her stories, and she finds joy in helping others achieve their own relationship with God. She is the founder of Women World Leaders, a ministry which empowers Women to find their beautiful PURPOSE God has designed for them.

Kimberly is married and lives in South Florida with her husband, where they own and operate their own financial coaching business. Together they share a heart for missions, serving consistently in South Africa. They take teams of people with them each year to introduce them to "serving others" overseas.

Kimberly is an established artist, with much of her work reaching across the country and around the world. She helps raise support for her mission passion projects and her 138 orphaned children she loves through Kerusglobal. org in South Africa.

Kimberly and her husband have three grown children as well as grandchildren and extended family in the State of Ohio. For more information or to contact Kimberly, please email her at Kimberly@womenworldleaders.com

The Beginning of Wisdom

KIMBERLY ANN HOBBS

Lord, help me to be the woman who fears you and finds favor in your eyes.

Charm is deceptive, and beauty is fleeting; but a woman who fears the Lord is to be praised (Proverbs 31:30).

How do we become the woman of virtue God intends us to be? We wish to walk in excellence, but it's not always easy. Personally, I can only lead by example and share with you that it is a day-by-day journey of crawling before walking and walking before running.

Have you ever asked God to do something major in your life and then experienced disappointment when He appeared to be working little-by-little rather than all at once?

God certainly has the power to give us instantaneous victories but often some of us take a lifetime before we see the activity we want. God is going by His timetable, not ours.

Despite my sometimes-impatient behavior, I can't imagine any place I'd rather be than centered in God's presence, exactly where He wants me. As a "woman of virtue," free from chains and bondage, I am now "walking in the excellence" of the abundant life my Savior has for me.

But… it wasn't always this way…

God tells us in Proverbs 9:10, NIV "The fear of the Lord is the beginning of wisdom."

Please walk back with me in time for just a moment. As a child I'm reflecting on the interior decor of my grandmother's old, cinderblock farmhouse. She had countless farm animals that roamed freely throughout her home. It was a sight to see. She had baby animal incubators, "hatcheries," in almost every room. It was quite interesting as a child to see live animals of different types mingled amidst her antiques, French Provincial and fine Italian furniture. I laugh as I think back. People nicknamed her "Ma Kettle" for her eccentric way of living. In her tiny kitchen on some old green linoleum sat a refrigerator. It was a pudgy, moss green-colored mass with two side-by-side front doors. Clutter covered the exposed greenish color. From top to bottom, newspaper clippings, old photographs, silly little magnets and handmade presents from "us children" smothered the exterior surface. But there was one thing that stands out in my mind to this day…it was taped on the far upper left corner of the freezer door and tiny in its size. It was something that remained perfectly in place on that refrigerator for 20-plus years: a teeny white paper which came from the inside of a fortune cookie. From the time I could remember—I was about seven years old—I would read the print on that paper every day that I slept at my Non's house. Each time I visited her, which was quite frequently, the paper never moved. On that paper were the words typed out in very small print: *The fear of the Lord is the beginning of wisdom.*

As years passed, I mentally saw those words become larger and more pronounced to me. As a child growing into adulthood, I read that tiny piece of paper hundreds if not thousands of times. It became a "beacon of light" on that old appliance. The POWER of God used that verse in my life and even though it was taken from a fortune cookie, God instilled the word "wisdom" into my soul.

God had imprinted "The fear of the Lord is the beginning of wisdom" into the depths of my being. When I found out later in life that the fortune was actually a Bible verse, it became even more profound to me. Little did my grandmother realize that her decision to tape up that small fortune from a cookie that she had received would result in a child gleaning depths of truth from it, something that would eventually change the direction of her life.

Reflecting on past stages of life, something like "walking in excellence" had been foreign to me. I wasn't sure how I'd get back on track to how close to God I was raised, given how far I had wandered. Unfortunately, distraction from God's path consumed many years of my life. My focus was on "me" and everything else around me, rather than the God I was supposed to love and serve but thankfully, I grew up understanding right and wrong. When I was good things went well and when I was bad, I was disciplined by parents or authority figures in my life. There were always consequences (often severe ones) for my bad behavior choices. Thankfully from a young age, my mom and grandmother were women of influence in my life. They taught me how to fear the Lord for my later days.

To fear God meant to reverence Him in a respectful way. I learned of this respect through discipline. I also learned about two forms of wisdom. There was Godly wisdom and then there was worldly wisdom. Making wise choices by useful knowledge in both areas was something I needed to learn. Unfortunately, I still made wrong choice after wrong choice in my earlier life, resulting in painful consequences.

I would often admire wise people as I began to grow older and I felt drawn into their conversations, gleaning the intensity of power they exemplified from their wise choices. I felt I lacked the knowledge that made me wise and I so badly desired it, and I began to study the behavior of these types of people. I found myself challenged to make better decisions and I did, sometimes. Still, in many areas of my life, my wrong choices continued to torment me.

Mistake after mistake, I was crying myself through life, feeling empty and void of knowledge. I was afraid of my future. I needed God's help to become one of the women I looked up to and admired—a woman of virtue, with the ability to walk through life with excellence.

Our Heavenly Father is working for our eternal good. He is accomplishing His purpose in our lives in His own perfect way, and in His own time. God's ways are not our ways and His thoughts are not our thoughts.

God knows that little steps are better for us where we are. He doesn't want us to be overwhelmed by situations that could happen if we experience them all too quickly and without learning from our mistakes, therefore He strengthens us, shapes us and rebuilds us from our errors of wrong choices.

As I pressed on in life, I reflected on the fortune paper and I began to pray about the word "wisdom"—the word I looked at for years on a refrigerator door. I definitely lacked wisdom in my life. Yes, I may have learned and yearned for worldly wisdom, having grasped only some of its meaning, but I knew what it was and wanted to obtain it, having lived among people who possessed it. I saw it in action around me and I even held on to some of it at times but I still continued to make those wrong choices.

Until...

Lying in bed one Spring day, I was very sick. I had been in bed for two weeks straight, suffering from a bout of severe depression. It was not something I had ever experienced before. I didn't care if I lived or died at this point. It was a scary place to be. I had made another serious mistake, a terrible mistake, and this time I did it while I was trying to walk with the Lord. How could I have done this? How could this have happened? I thought I surrendered all to Jesus. I was following him. How could this be? I was doing everything I thought to be right but I messed up again. Why?

James 1:5, NIV says, "If any of you lacks wisdom, you should ask God, who gives generously without finding fault, and it will be given to you."

I never asked Him for it! It was that simple.

I needed godly wisdom, the wisdom He spoke of throughout His Word. That Word that showed up on a refrigerator almost daily throughout my life was the answer, but how could I finally grasp it? I laid in that bed regretting my life and lamenting over another painful mistake. God had to speak to me in the darkness of that room and show me what I was lacking all along.

Prayer is the way we find God's wisdom. There is no other wisdom I wish to possess than the godly wisdom that now directs my every step in my life.

A ray of sunlight shone through a crack in the curtains as I lay in that dark room in my bed. The ray of light was peeping through the dark curtain right on God's word. The Bible lay open on the bed that afternoon, as I had intentions to try and read for a bit.

God told me at that moment, I had to pray for it. He also told me I could not do things on my own any longer. I needed to ask for the James 1:5 wisdom He spoke of.

So I got it. I understood it and I began to pray. For three years I made it routine, praying that prayer before my feet touched the ground each day. I asked God out loud and repeatedly for the wisdom he spoke of in James 1:5. I placed that verse on mirrors in my home and on walls throughout my house. I spoke that verse back to him continuously, over and over and for months on end.

God began to reach into the depths of my soul and implant wisdom. His wisdom. It wasn't instantaneous but it was a progression of correct choices. My daily prayers for wisdom eventually began to reveal daily progress. My life changed.

Please be encouraged that even in the tiniest of increments, God is at work in your life as you ask Him to be. Be assured He will work within as you surrender yourself daily to Him. He will begin to work through your life and through the lives of those around you. You will find as I did that little by little this will all add up to major change in your life.

Fearing God brought me to understanding godly wisdom and my lack of it. If we lack God's wisdom, we will just continue trying to get through life in our own strength and with our own understanding. This doesn't make for the abundant life God has for us. By lacking godly wisdom, we end up making wrong decisions and doing ungodly things.

I became so frustrated with my foolish choices it led me to pain and heartache. The continuous unhealthy pattern led me to the fear of what God was going to do with me. God wasn't punishing me, not at all; I was only suffering from consequences of my own stupid choices and I needed to stop. I eventually did stop when I fully surrendered and asked for His wisdom. I cried out to God for the wisdom I saw all those years on the refrigerator door, and He began to give it to me.

Praying daily for godly wisdom became easy for me because God told me I needed to ask Him for it and so I did. Once I did, my life changed.

Pray for wisdom. You will find yourself doing things so wise, you may even be surprised. You will make a decision that turns out to be so completely right that you will be amazed. You will have insight like you've never had before. Trust God; He honors His Words.

You will begin to give sound advice to people who ask for it. You will sense danger when it's lurking. You will know when to speak and when not to speak. You'll know what to say and how to say it. You will have a sense of what to do and what not to do in any situation, and please allow me to write one more thought: There is no other wisdom that you should long for over godly wisdom. It was the only thing King Solomon asked God for, and he was the wisest man in history.

As a woman of virtue, walking in excellence, God has led me to work with women now on a daily basis. I share my mistakes but I share the wisdom God has planted and grown within me so as not to continue those mistakes. God gave me a vision to lead a multitude of women with love and encouragement into finding their beautiful purpose.

As I gained godly wisdom, He has brought me in front of women from around the world. I am able to pour into their lives, one by one, as God leads me through a process. God is pouring His wisdom out on me, I pour it out to them and what God is now doing is exceedingly, abundantly beyond imagination (Ephesians 3:20).

This group of women I have the privilege to lead is spreading around the globe like wildfire across a dry field. Women World Leaders is becoming a movement and it's all by God's power working within women who are making wise choices, women who are asking the Holy Spirit to lead them each day as they serve. They are women of virtue, walking in excellence, but they are fully surrendered now to do so.

Anything can be accomplished when God is present. Ephesians 3:20 is my life verse. I carry it and deposit it wherever I am led:

"Now to him who is able to do exceedingly abundantly above all we could ask or imagine; according to the power at work within us."

God showed up when I asked Him to. The power of the Holy Spirit began to work in my daily life because I asked Him to. It wasn't always like this. I had to make a choice, a determination to stop making the wrong decisions and ask God for wisdom to make the right ones. You can pause and ask God at this moment for His wisdom. He will give it to you because He promised He would in His Word, and generously.

There is no time like the present to ask for wisdom because you're never too young and never too old. When you receive it, you will begin to walk in excellence each day and in time, God's time, you will become a life-changer. No longer did I want to be a life-sucker another moment, feeling the life leave my body each time I made a horrible mistake. I became unbearable to live with.

I challenge you to become a woman of virtue and walk in excellence and godly wisdom. Allow God to show you any pride that may be hiding in your life, and whenever He does, confess it to Him as sin and acknowledge Him as Lord over every area of your life.

This must become a daily reaching for you in surrendering yourself to the Lord. Ask God for the ability to see your trials as strengthening times in your life. Ask Him to make you more like Christ and to enable you to handle the working tasks that He presents to you. When women come to me and ask for coaching, I feel it blesses me more than them because I know God sent them to me to encourage them.

Daily we need to ask the Holy Spirit to control our tongues. Everything we say should reflect godly wisdom and our love for Jesus. Remember, our tongues are untamable by human effort, so ask God to protect your tongue each day as you start out (James 3:8).

God gives wisdom generously to any of us who ask, and it's so rewarding. I receive daily blessings because God allows me the ability to pour wisdom out to women everywhere. It's no longer about me but godly wisdom working through me to point others directly to Him. I feel as though I live in a puffy cloud of cushioned blessings all around me.

I can't stop asking God for His wisdom each day because I would never want to think I made my "own" decision ever again. I'm much more confident in life knowing its God's decision, not my own. I wish always to please Him, to be the woman of virtue walking in excellence because God is pouring His wisdom out on me. I simply pray and ask, pray and ask, pray and ask over everything before my day even begins.

The prayers of the righteous are powerful and effective (James 5:16); how can we deny this?

Whatever work we do as women of virtue, we should want to do it well and be successful. When our work is good, it gives us fulfillment. When we accomplish something worthwhile, it makes life better for other people and our families and ourselves. It gives us all satisfaction.

The ideal woman described in the Bible in Proverbs 31 is a hard worker. She buys and sells; she plants vineyards; she makes clothing and she sells it; she is a woman of strength energy and vision. She works long into the night and knows what she has to offer is very good. God wants us to experience that type of success and satisfaction but it doesn't happen without:

- Fearing God
- Seeking Godly wisdom
- Praying for Godly wisdom and asking Him for it

Be diligent in these areas, and the rewards will come when you do the work God brings about inside your life.

Whether it's maintaining a home, serving at a rescue mission or committing to a ministry, or even teaching a young child to tie his shoes or caring for the sick and elderly, your reward for seeing the "results of your labor" is priceless.

Ask God for wisdom to direct you. Pray and commit your work to the Lord, and He will bless it.

"Commit to the LORD whatever you do, **and your plans will succeed"** (Proverbs 16:3, NIV)

No matter what your paycheck reflects, your work is important to God. It's important to others and it's important to you. Don't give up. Strive to be that woman of virtue others admire. Give others incentive that they can achieve this by asking it of God.

"Remember, charm is deceptive and beauty is fleeting; But a woman who fears the Lord is to be praised" (Proverbs 31:30, NIV),

~and~

"The fear of the Lord is the beginning of wisdom" (Proverbs 9:10, NIV).

Become a "wise woman of God" and lead the world.

Waiting for the Other Shoe to Drop...but God Built My Strength!

JENNIFER BRYANT

My story walks you through my journey of being a Proverbs woman while facing deaths of those close to me. Although my upbringing in a Pentecostal church provided me with a religious foundation, it wasn't enough to help me through the trauma I faced in life. Waiting for something traumatic to happen was inevitable and that negative thought process became a part of my daily mindset. Why couldn't I live life without thinking about the next traumatic event that would raise my anxieties? Why couldn't I rejoice during those happy times? My answer was because I was always waiting for the other shoe to drop...but God showed himself within me to trust the process while he built my character, wisdom, courage, and strength. It took time for me to mature in the Lord and cultivate those virtues in my life. I often meditated on Philippians 4:5-6, "Don't worry about anything: instead, pray about everything; tell God your needs and don't forget to thank him for his answers. If you do this you will experience God's peace, which is far more wonderful than the human mind can understand."

I'll share several pivotal points in my life where I had to trust God throughout the process. The journey I traveled wasn't easy after experiencing the deaths of immediate family and one of my best friends. All these sudden deaths added another level of complication to my psyche because I was left with many questions. I went through the stages of grief and couldn't process them fully because death came knocking again before I could process the previous one. I was very sad and it took all of my strength to continue life because death consumed me all the time.

A DAUGHTER'S FIRST LOVE DIED

I can recall how my dad would be so protective over me at the age of five. Every day when he came home from work, he would call out my name after he greeted my mom. He would carefully watch the way my brother would deal with me. I felt his love at such a young age. My life changed forever at the age of five when two men walked down the sidewalk approaching our apartment building while my brother was peering out the window watching them. The men knocked on the door, and delivered the news that my dad would not return home EVER again. They delivered the news that there was a construction accident and my dad was crushed by a one-ton pipe due to a crane malfunction while it was being lowered into a ditch where he worked. My mom looked so confused when she received the news and moments later the men asked her to accompany them to go identify her 28-year-old husband. Wait...what just happened? My mom, with a fifth grade education and no job, had to quickly figure out how she would raise two children on her own. That's when my life changed forever...

WHERE'S MY MOM?

We temporarily moved in with one of my aunts until my mom could save enough money to move us to a two-bedroom apartment. My mother was a virtuous, strong, and graceful woman who attended church all the time. She always was neatly dressed, with pretty dresses and suits adorned with beautiful, shiny jewelry. Her behavior and actions aligned with all of the qualities of a virtuous woman. While in my senior year in high school and shortly after she remarried, I noticed that my mom lost her drive and she began behaving oddly. I suspect that she suppressed my dad's traumatic death for so many years, until she remarried. My only sibling, my brother, couldn't help me with her because he was incarcerated. It took me a while to build trust with my stepdad because he wasn't always present while my mom was dating him because he was dealing with his demon of alcoholism. Our relationship grew once he got saved.

Mom had many manic episodes including feeling euphoric, having more energy than usual, insomnia, jumbled thoughts, feeling irritable, and doing risky things. During her spells of insomnia, she would wander off in the woods. She would go on extreme buying sprees, and then throw away all the clothes the same day. She gave away thousands of dollars to family members and friends. She would open our apartment window and throw away cash daily while people would laugh and wait for the next time to get money from a woman who couldn't help herself. My heart was hurting for her. I didn't know what to do. She was delusional and had several narratives that were untrue going on inside her head. One night she threw bullets against my door and told me if I tried to poison her again, she would kill me. She thought she miscarried a set of twins, but was never pregnant. She went through a phase of being a man. She walked and dressed like one.

I left my home immediately because I was concerned about my safety and thought I could help her better living outside the home. I was an emotional wreck. I constantly walked around with anxiety. Even to this day, I wonder how I maintained honor roll and was successful in my career. I faced such loneliness during my senior year in high school while I was taking care of my mom and working a part time job at a fast food restaurant.

The day I discovered she died once was when the psychiatrist shared with me that she had an extreme case of bipolar disorder and schizophrenia, and in spite of her medications, including antipsychotics and antidepressants, she would never be the same. My hurt for her ran deep because she was suffering and I couldn't make the pain stop for her. She isolated herself. Family and friends rarely came around because they were afraid of her and didn't understand the disease. I couldn't place a Band-Aid on her pain because what was going on was much bigger than a cut. She would be fine for a few months, and then convince herself that she didn't need the meds anymore. The cycle of her manic depression was so exhausting. I could tell her loving second husband was growing tired too. We became a team and got her to the best state possible. I realized the mother I knew wasn't coming back. "Rest assured," I promised her husband, my step dad, "I will not stop helping her, and I will not leave you alone through this situation." I never thought the next traumatic event I faced was real.

A PRECIOUS ANGEL GONE

One week after my husband and I celebrated our one-year wedding anniversary, I came home from a long day of work and saw a note on the door addressed to my husband from a Maryland State

Trooper. He called the number, and never did I think his next words to me would be that his three-year-old daughter who lived in North Carolina died in a car crash, and her mother was unconscious in the hospital, and her sibling survived with scratches. His daughter was the only one who died in the car. We traveled to North Carolina to identify her body and buried her during the flood of 1999. That was a life-changing event in itself. Our marriage was never the same from that profound loss that will be remembered daily. I began to ask God why she was the only one to die. Was I prepared for what would come next?

MY MOTHER'S DEATH

I came home after a long day at work. My husband at the time told me he wanted to take me out for a late-night dinner. I thought that was strange because we had spoken earlier that day about cooking the homemade hamburger patties I made with all the seasonings and onions locked in. We had spoken that morning about all we needed were the buns. What changed our plans? He knew I wasn't a big fan of late dinners and taking the girls off their schedules during the week. I asked him where we would take the girls. He said to his mom's house. The ride to his mom's house was quiet and eerie. I felt in my spirit something wasn't right. We pulled into the parking space at his mom's apartment complex. He took the girls inside while I waited in the SUV.

He came out and we sat there and I asked him why we weren't leaving to go get something to eat. He grabbed my hand, and he said, "I have something to tell you." My heart was beating very fast. His next words were, "Your mom passed away today." I said, "You're kidding, right? I just called her this morning to tell her that I was

coming back this week because we had such a great time last week."
My last time with her was the best time in a long time and she had
told me she loved me, and that was rare. I asked how she died. He
said she died from choking while eating and had collapsed on top
of my bonus dad. In my mind, I was saying, *This can't be true.*

Immediately, I asked him to take me to the hospital so I could see
her. The hospital staff was so kind and allowed me to go to the
morgue to see her. She looked like she was sleeping peacefully. It
was like time stood still for a very long time. I couldn't believe my
mom was lying there like she was asleep. I kept saying "wake up" in
my mind. She was gone at the age of 61. Another traumatic moment
where I questioned God: "Hello, are you there? Why are you doing
this to me? How long will it be before the other shoe drops?"

OH NO! NOT ONE OF MY CLOSEST FRIENDS...

Two years after my mom's death, I received a phone call that one of
my closest friends had suddenly died. I recall her mom called me
from her phone. I thought my best friend was following up with
me about rescheduling our movie date. Immediately, I answered,
"Girl, when are we going to the movies?" I heard her mom on the
other end of the phone saying, "She died today." I couldn't believe
what I had heard. I bellowed out so loudly, "Oh no, oh no," and
dropped to the floor, weeping. I could barely walk down the aisle in
church when seeing her lying in the casket. My palms were sweaty,
my knees were shaking, and I sat there numb. After her funeral,
I couldn't snap out of it. I dreamed about her death and saw how
she died, which sank me deeper into depression because I hurt
because I couldn't help her. I lost hope, and my mind was overly
consumed with death throughout the day. I missed her dearly, and

each time I visited my mom's gravesite to place flowers, I would also place flowers on her grave that was nearby. The cycle of imagining my death returned. I dreamed about my death. I talked about my death. What was there to live for anymore? I had experienced another traumatic loss, and my marriage was failing. I might as well wait for the shoe to drop again! Who would be next - me?

GIRL, GET IT TOGETHER...

My recovery period from the sudden death of my mom and closest friend was slow. One day while feeling isolated and alone sitting on my couch, I texted my closest friends and family, letting them know I was depressed and that I was going to see a psychiatrist and therapist. I didn't want to live again. I was overwhelmed and my recovery period was long. I held a senior position at work and was a mother of two and a wife. I would come home exhausted because I was trying to maintain perfection while hiding my depression. I would try to drown out the noise inside my head and the negative stories with gospel music, wine, and food. I know it sounds like an odd combination. I was trying to make this pain go away.

When I got home after work, I would go to my room, sleep, wake up and repeat the routine. I isolated myself from my family. I was in a robotic, functional depressed state and I felt like no one was coming to save me, and people were tired of hearing my sad stories. My doctor prescribed me Celexa for two years to help with my anxiety and depression. While weaning myself off the medication under the doctor's care, I had a major setback and thought I was going to die because my thoughts were so deep and I felt like I was in an abyss so deep, and I questioned why I should continue to live. I began to journal more. I began to pray more. I began to

139

surround myself with positive people and recognized the power of protecting my energy. Then I was reminded by God...Genesis 50:24, NKJV "And Joseph said to his brethren, 'I am dying; but God will surely visit you, and bring you out of this land to the land of which He swore to Abraham, Isaac, and Jacob'" and Psalm 73:26, NIV "My flesh and my heart fail; But God is the strength of my heart and my portion forever." I began to regain strength until I lost my last living grandmother, the woman who always told me things would be okay. You may think the deaths I experienced were a natural part of life. Maybe, but the timing of them was hard for me. Daily I would walk around reciting to myself, Isaiah 54:17, KJV "No weapon formed against thee shall prosper!"

Yet again, I went back into the cycle of waiting for the other shoe to drop. Who's next to go?

MY BROTHER'S KEEPER

My 49-year-old brother, my only sibling, dealt with heart failure two years before his death. During one of his hospital stays, the doctor allowed me to listen to his heart murmur and leaking valve. His pumping blood flowing to his heart sounded like turbulent, gushing water leaking. His prognosis was bleak but the doctor said his life could be prolonged if he had open-heart surgery, took better care of himself, took his medicine, and kept his doctor's appointments. He grew tired of the doctors and was afraid to "get his chest cracked open," as he described it. The last 30 days of my brother's life were eye–opening for both of us. While we didn't know it was his last 30 days, we made the best of those days. Two weeks before his death, I dreamed about it. God was trying to prepare me for it, and I wasn't giving up on my brother's life. I visited him every day in the hospital while he was waiting for his scheduled open-heart surgery, and I was growing concerned about him but couldn't let him see it.

During the 30 days, we reflected on funny childhood memories, his earlier days of using and selling drugs, his walk with God later in life, his love for his family, and his ministering work to those in prison. We talked about his absence during my lifetime, especially during times I needed him. All wrongs were mutually forgiven. I remember his fears and concerns of being transported from one hospital in Prince George's County to another one in Baltimore, MD where his surgery would take place. He promised he would call me when it was time to move because he knew I wanted to be there. I was anxious so I called him and he said they hadn't given him a time for his surgery yet. I went to sleep.

I woke up the next morning, looked at my phone, and noticed he left me a voice message around 2:04 a.m. stating he was getting transported. Worry consumed me because I hadn't heard from him again that morning. I researched which hospital he was transported to in Baltimore and I called the head nurse. She asked me if he was married because she noticed his wedding ring. I thought to myself, *why would she ask me that and why didn't she ask him?* My anxious heart began palpitating really quickly. I told her he was married and gave his wife's information. The nurse told me she would have to call his wife and that she couldn't give me any information. I called his wife and told her that the nurse would be calling her and asked her to call me back after she'd spoken to the head nurse at the hospital. She called me back to tell me that he had stopped breathing. Wait, what? Wait...you're kidding, right? Not again...what am I supposed to do with that information? I went to the hospital and saw all the tubes were attached to him. I couldn't believe what I was seeing. I spent the night at the hospital praying for a good outcome and that he would wake up. He was in the same state the next day. His wife called me to say he died. My only sibling was gone. I went into shock. After my brother's death, I felt that life had no meaning and wished to be released from the pain or to join my other family members.

Be careful what you ask for and watch your thought process...

NEAR DEATH EXPERIENCE

In 2016, while traveling with my daughters to get food, my gas light came on due to a faulty new fuel pump in my Jeep, which caused it to stop without warning in the center lane on the busy Capital Beltway. A tractor trailer nearly hit my Jeep and my daughters and I were very scared. I started calling on the mighty name of Jesus several times, asking Him to help us. My daughters' faces looked horrified when they looked out the rear-view mirror and saw the truck quickly approaching. My oldest daughter said she was asking God to not allow the crash to be too painful while my youngest daughter was screaming how scared she was. For the first time, I felt like I could not protect my children from danger. All I could do was rely on my faith while rubbing the ring on my necklace that my grandmother had given me. But God stepped in and the tractor trailer moved to the next lane in record time. A tow truck was behind us in the center lane. When he saw my disabled Jeep, he pulled in front of us and said he witnessed that we almost lost our lives and that he came to save our lives. He brought us home safely. I became overprotective to my children and jumped into helicopter mom mode while also becoming needy in my relationships, and some of my romantic relationships were unhealthy because I was yearning for love and fearful of loss. I went back to the therapist and church to strengthen my walk with Christ and deepen my faith.

"Anxiety weighs down the heart, but a kind word cheers it up." (Proverbs 12:25, NIV)

A NEW ME - A VIRTUOUS WOMAN WHO CELEBRATES LIFE

My losses gave me a different perspective. I shifted my mindset while in my executive leadership program at American University. I went to lunch with my executive coach, who said to me, "You've spent your life caring for others. You are living your life waiting for the other shoe to drop. You are guarded, and a closed fist will not allow anything or anyone in it." I cried; she was right. That was an AHA moment for me to reflect and think about my purpose in life. I had the courage to look fear in the eye and said, "You can't live here anymore because my purpose in life is to inspire others." I was inspired to ignite my fire to share my story with others who may be despondent about their situations, and I became a co-facilitator for a ministry at my church to build up other women by cultivating deep, meaningful, nurturing relationships with them as they work through life challenges. I celebrate my life and my loving friends and family.

"Strength and honor are her clothing; and she shall rejoice in time to come." (Proverbs 31:25, KJV)

Becoming a Proverbs 31 woman is about embracing God's grace, bearing God's image, and fulfilling God's call for my life. It isn't easy and is something that should be practiced daily, no matter where you are in your walk with God or in life. I have had my share of disappointments, including being fatherless during my childhood and spending my teenage years caring for a mentally ill mother during a time when my only sibling was incarcerated. After going through domestic abuse and sexual assaults in two different relationships during my twenties before marriage, ending an 18-year marriage, losing my stepdaughter, my mom, one of my best friends, my paternal grandmother, and suffering from depression, I was ready to live life without regrets. I got lost in a cycle of obsessing about death. I was longing for freedom and relief from those thoughts. I had to get rid of the fear of abandonment because of the deaths of those close to me. It wasn't an easy process and there were times that I was secretly feeling unworthy. I would numb my feelings by eating and drinking too much, overspending, going into unhealthy relationships, and staying insanely busy. I spent considerable time working on myself and my anxieties, recognizing "red flags" in relationships sooner, asking the right questions, and establishing boundaries. I asked God for forgiveness and I forgave myself. Even when I failed, God's grace helped put me back on track. I learned to trust the process to unchain myself from the cycle. I no longer lived in my secret hell of depression. I reminded myself that God didn't leave me on earth without a purpose. That purpose was to go through my process and help others by speaking the truth and earning the trust of others through my authenticity, transparency, and relatability.

Natural death is real. I was alive and dead on the inside, and had to reach within to regain my power through God's help to create a "new normal" for my life.

"Who can find a virtuous woman for her price is far above rubies." (Proverbs 31:10, KJV)

You must go through the healing process in your own way to become a virtuous woman. It is not a matter of checking off a list of accomplishments to attain the perfection of virtuous women in the Bible. Rather, it is studying the virtues and living a life where they are evident. No, you don't have to wear a big sign on your chest that reads, "I'm a virtuous woman." You model the behavior, forgive others, and reach back to mentor others.

As a retired federal executive and currently a life and career coach, I recognize that women need mentors. We need support to stand in our power. With each determination to bounce back, your capacity to bounce back grows stronger through forgiveness and God's grace and mercy. The raw experience of living in the moment with a deep sense of connection with God can be powerful and liberating because you know He has your back. Through God's grace we can conquer anything! Going through my life experiences has caused me to reflect and think about my purpose in life, and it has inspired me to ignite my fire to share my story with others who may be despondent about their situations and let them know they can make it too.

Muriel Caroline Grooms was born May 1964 to Mr. Nathaniel and the late Mrs. Treola Grooms (2011). She is the third of four children born to my mom and dad. She has two older sisters and one younger brother. She also has other sisters and brothers (three are deceased) by her father. She has two daughters, and three grandchildren. She was blessed with another brother who was born my cousin, raised as my uncle, but, in my eyes, has always been my big brother, the honorable Odell Grooms, two brothers-in-law, and two sisters-in-law.

Muriel was born and raised in, SE Washington, DC, Anacostia. She lived in the DC, Maryland area all her life until June 2018 when she moved to Knightdale, NC. She attended, Ketchum Elementary, Kramer Jr. High, and Anacostia Senior High, all in SE, Washington, DC. She also attended the Smith Business School, and Jefferson Business College. She joined the Federal Government, US Government Accountability Office, January 1989, where she is still employed today. She is looking forward to retirement, May 2020.

In addition to writing, she has been singing all her life. She is a member of an awesome ministry, Alvin Campbell and Total Praise, her nephew, Alvin Campbell, Jr., founder. They are currently in the studio recording their third project. Look for its release very soon.

Having therefore obtained help of God, I continue unto this day… (Acts 26:22, KJV)

I Do...

MURIEL GROOMS

"I, ___, take thee, ___, to be my wedded husband/wife, to have and to hold, from this day forward, for better, for worse, for richer, for poorer, in sickness and in health, to love and to cherish, till death do us part, according to God's holy ordinance; and thereto I pledge thee my faith [or] pledge myself to you."

Those are the words we say, the commitment we make, the confession, the vows, and covenant to make to our mate before God, our families, and friends. But do we read these vows and understand them before we say "I do?" When you're standing there at the altar everything, in most cases, is wonderful. We're so happy just thinking about how wonderful our lives will be with our forever love. I don't think we're thinking about the fact that this person or you may get sick and you will have to be their caretaker. How long are you willing to do that? We say forever in our vows. Wikipedia says, "In the time of the Roman Empire (17 BC – 476 AD) the lower classes had 'free' marriages. The bride's father would deliver her to the groom, and the two agreed that they were wed and would keep the vow of marriage by mutual consent. Wealthy Romans, though, would sign documents listing property rights to publicly declare that their union was legalized and not a common law marriage. This was the beginning of the official recording of marriage.

"The oldest traditional wedding vows can be traced back to the manuals of the medieval church. In England, there were manuals of the dioceses of Salisbury (Sarum) and York. The compilers of the first Book of Common Prayer, published in 1549, based its marriage service mainly on the Sarum manual. Upon agreement to marry, the Church of England usually offered couples a choice. The couple could promise each other to 'love and cherish' or, alternatively, the groom promises to 'love, cherish, and worship,' and the bride to 'love, cherish, and obey.'"

A lot of things have changed and there are all kinds of marriages and relationships these days. But God creates; matches are made in heaven. He said, "Let there be light. The light was day and the darkness He called night, GOOD. God created a firmament to separate the water from the waters. He called the firmament Heaven, GOOD. God created the Earth, grass, trees, and the seas, GOOD. God created the seasons, years, days, sun, moon, and the stars, GOOD. He created the fowl and the great whale, GOOD. God created the beast, the cattle, and the creeping things, GOOD. Then God formed man out of the dust of the ground. And the Lord God formed man of the dust of the ground and breathed into his nostrils the breath of life; and man became a living soul" (Genesis 2:7, NIV). "The Lord God planted a garden (Eden) and placed the man in it. Every tree was pleasant to the sight. The tree of life [was] in the midst of the garden, and the tree of knowledge of good and evil. He created the river to water the garden in four heads, Pison, Gihon, Hiddekel, and Euphrates. The man was to dress it and keep it. And then God said, NOT GOOD. God didn't want man to be alone. And the Lord God said, it is not good that the man should be alone; I will make him an help meet for him. (Genesis 2:18, KJV). He made a woman and brought her unto the man.

HELP MEET: Amplified Bible version: one who balances him—a counterpart; like his opposite. There are other Bible versions, "a helper fit for him" (RSV), "a helper as his partner" (NRS), "a helper comparable to him" (NKJ) and "a helper as his counterpart" (YLT). The Lord made a woman opposite the man, yet in agreement with the man, to help the man. The Lord God put them together. A match made in Heaven.

Why do we get married? Do you think there would be as many weddings as there are if we spent time on the answer to that question before the wedding? Do you think there would be as many weddings if the Lord God put them together? If we spent as much time on why as we spend on the preparations for the wedding, most of us probably wouldn't get married. What is it that attracts us to it? I think it's love in most cases. We want to have that life partner that will love and grow with us forever. That's a wonderful thing. Who wouldn't want that? But how do we know that the other person or even you will want to be with that person FOREVER? Why that person? Did the Lord God put you together? What is it about them that makes you want to say I'll spend FOREVER with you? Is it just because you love them? Do you really love them? Love is intense, not just a word; it's not just a feeling. Love is an action. "**Love suffers long and is kind; love does not envy; love does not parade** itself, is not puffed up; does not behave rudely, does not seek its own, is not provoked, thinks no **evil**; does not rejoice in iniquity, but rejoices in the truth; bears all things, believes all things, hopes all things, endures all things. **Love never fails.**" (1 Corinthians 13:4-8, NKJV). Love is the greatest.

Look at your relationship. Can you say now that you'll have this true love 10 or 15 years from now? Not the feeling of love, true love. Are you willing to love, truly love this person forever? Do you like the person you're with? What don't you like about them? Are you willing to live with those dislikes forever? Remember, you're not only saying yes to the good, you're also saying yes to the not so good. Can you just sit and be with this person? What are your life's goals? What do you want to accomplish in life? What is your five- or ten-year plan? Do you want children? Do you want to go to school or back to school? Do you want to travel? What's your credit looking like? Do you want to invest? When will you retire? Are you willing to relocate? Are you going to make a career change? What are you both like when you're angry? How do you handle or resolve conflict? What's he like when he's sick? Can you pray for him/her? Will you pray for them? There are a trillion and one questions that can be asked. These questions are very important because you have got to agree. "Can two walk together, except they be agreed" (Amos 3:3, KJV) I don't know if they all can be answered before "I do" but these questions have got to be addressed.

The two of you will be one, one flesh. "For this cause shall a man leave his father and mother, and cleave to his wife; and they twain shall be one flesh: so, then they are no more twain, but one flesh. What therefore God hath joined together, let not man put asunder (apart; divided)" (Mark 10:7-9, KJV). You would look real crazy fighting yourself. Does this mean you're always going to agree on everything all the time? No, but you're not going to be disagreeable. You can resolve issues and circumstances with an agreeable spirit, with a loving heart and in a loving manner. You're looking for an agreement, not an argument. It's not about who's right or wrong. It's about what's best for the two of you and your living in peace. He may have to correct you sometimes and you may not like it at the time; that's okay. You take the correction in love because if he loves you that's how he's giving the correction—in love. You may even get a little angry. That's okay too if you get over it quickly. Don't go to bed angry.

There's no reason to have anger, hard feelings and conflict lingering in a relationship. You just want to live in peace and harmony with each other. "Be ye angry, and sin not: let not the sun go down upon your wrath" (Ephesians 4:26, KJV).

What has God already spoken about this union? "Whoso findeth a wife finds a good thing, and obtaineth favour (approval, support) of the Lord" (Proverbs 18:22, NKJV). Are you already a wife? Are you a help meet? "Wives, submit yourselves unto your own husbands, as unto the Lord" (Ephesians 5:22, NIV). The Amplified Bible says the wife is to be subject to her husband, not to men in general; not as inferior to him, nor in violation of her Christian ethics, but honoring her husband as protector and head of the home, respecting the responsibility of his position and his accountability to God. Many women see that word, submit, and they resist, but we have got to submit and be subject to our husbands just as we submit to God. Maybe that's the problem: We're not submissive to God. We are to be subject and submissive to the Lord our God so that we can be subject to our own husbands before "I do." Marriage is not something to rush into. Marriage is a forever commitment. We have got to respect and reverence the man as the head. The wife must respect and delight in her husband, notice him and prefer him and treat him with loving concern, treasuring him, honoring him, and holding him dear.

"The husband is the head of the wife, even as Christ is the head of the church: and he is the saviour of the body" (Ephesians 5:23, KJV). Husbands are to love their wives just like Christ loved the church. That's a command. Husbands love! Christ sanctified and cleansed the church. The husband is obligated to love his wife just as his own body. Look for the good for her; give her caring, unselfish love. He is to nourish, protect, and love her just as Christ loves the church. Love her with behavior worthy of respect and esteem, always seeking the best for her with an attitude of lovingkindness.

Man, woman, husband, wife, are you READY?

We can take as much time as we need to make sure we are ready to commit to this forever covenant. The Lord God Almighty created—six days, He created. God is not governed by time, but He took six days to create. He took His time. He could have spoken and everything—heavens, earth, trees, grass, animals, everything—could have appeared at once, but He took His time. Take your time.

We spend a lot of time and money investing in people and the wedding without taking the time before the relationship, the marriage, looking hard at our ever-after. How much time do you spend with yourself and God? Are you always surrounded by others? What's your quiet time like? What do you know about yourself? How much time do you spend in devotion with the Lord God? What's your prayer life like? "He that is unmarried careth for the things that belong to the Lord, how he may please the Lord" (1 Corinthians 7:32, KJV). Are you too busy? Are you making time for the Lord? Do you have time for a partner? There are many things to consider before "I do," and both of you have got to examine yourselves first. If this person is the person for you, and they want to be with you just as much as you want to be with them, they'll take the time it takes to have a great forever-after.

Marriage should be a wonderful thing. I've heard many wonderful love stories. It is God-ordained and everything the Lord God does He does well. "The blessing of the Lord, it maketh rich, and he addeth no sorrow with it" (Proverbs 10:22, KJV). We can't go wrong with a God foundation. It is a solid foundation that will never fail; it lasts forever. Be happy forever, married or not.

I'm not an expert. I'm not a counselor, MD, PhD, or any of those things. I am, however, one who was married and now I am not. I will never say I failed at love because love never fails. I had to take a good look at me. Was I really ready for forever love? A lot of the questions I asked in this chapter I had to ask myself. The problem is I didn't ask myself these questions before I said, "I do." I had never spent a lot of time alone with myself before I said, "I do." If you desire to be married, great! In the meantime, live your life. Get to know you. Build a great relationship with the Lord God. Put Him first in your life and let Him reveal true love to you. "But seek ye first the kingdom of God, and His righteousness; and all these things shall be added unto you" (Matthew 6:33, KJV).

Stevie Wonder wrote a song titled, "As." It is deep. I don't know who he was thinking about when he wrote the song, but that's some kind of love.

Nobody can love you like the Lord God loves you. His love is amazing, breathtaking, out of this world. Our mortal minds will never comprehend His love for us. When you get all wrapped up in His love you won't desire or accept anything less. All He wants is what's best for us. You can trust in Him. He will never fail us. There's no greater love than the love of Jesus. "For God so loved the world, that He gave His only begotten Son, that whosoever believeth in Him should not perish, but have everlasting life" (John 3:16, KJV). God, with all His wonder and might, loves us enough to die for us. He took on a fleshly body, Jesus, so He could live on earth and die just to save us. He didn't just die, He suffered. They spit on Him, slapped Him, punched Him with their fists; He was severely whipped; they mocked and ridiculed Him, and twisted thorns and put them on His head.

They struck Him repeatedly on the head with a reed (a long bamboo-like stick). He was stripped of His clothes. They put nails in His hands and feet. He took on all the suffering, hurt, defeat, sickness, confusion, disease, heartbreak—everything. He hung on the cross for three hours, suffered for three hours, all because He loves us. Crucifixion isn't an easy death. It is said that when crucified a person could expect to live for no more than 24 hours. Jesus suffered for three hours. "The weight of the body pulling down on the arms makes breathing extremely difficult," said Jeremy Ward, physiologist at King's College London.

Crucifixion, suffocation, loss of body fluids and multiple organ failures—Jesus endured it all for us. He did it for all of us because He loves all of us, even the crowd that yelled, "Crucify Him, crucify Him." He knew that some of us would reject Him. He knew that His dying would mean absolutely nothing to some. He knew some wouldn't believe and would never accept Him. But He still loved us enough to die for us. Even while He was suffering on the cross, people were yelling at Him, mocking Him. He said, "Father, forgive them; for they do not know what they are doing" (Luke 23:34, AMP). He never stopped thinking about us. He never stopped loving us. That's love. That's true love. It really blows my mind as I think of all this. It brings tears to my eyes to think that someone loves me that much. WOW! What kind of love it this? It's forever love. It's a love that will never end. It's a love that is faithful and true. So why would we settle for anything less? He should be our foundation and guide for not just marriage, but for our lives.

155

Marriage is honorable in all, and the bed undefiled: but whore-mongers and adulterers God will judge. (Hebrews 13:4, KJV)

"Love is not false dependency nor attempts to control the other. Love means giving of ourselves—freely." - Bishop T.D. Jakes

"Love is composed of a single soul inhabiting two bodies." - Aristotle

"A wise woman helps her husband succeed. She keeps asking him questions, studies her husband. Struggles to get his vision and his dreams. A stupid woman criticizes her husband. An ideal woman is a helper, and you cannot help someone without knowing his vision. Help the man." - Myles Munroe

"Do you know how you tell real love? It's when someone else's interest trumps your own." - Brad Pitt

"God did not create woman from man's head, that he should command her, nor from his feet, that she should be his slave, but rather from his side, that she should be near his heart." - Myles Munroe

I do! Do you???

"Therefore what God

has joined together,

let no one separate."

(Mark 10:9, NIV)

Briana C. CaBell is a young woman moved to walk in her gifting. Briana has been writing since early childhood and though suffering many emotional strongholds in her life, attributes her God-given writing ability in helping her overcome.

Ms. CaBell published her first of many books at the age of 25. In ensuing years, she continued to publish books while working in ministry, writing, producing and directing, running a catering business and furthering her education.

In 2017 Briana established Elohim Multimedia to publish and promote her work and the works of others. In 2018 Briana was granted a new opportunity. Using her nickname, she began hosting a radio show called The UpLIFT Show w/ Breezy which airs weekly on the Stellar Award nominated Awesome God Radio.

Ms. CaBell cites not her personal strength but strong faith and strong support for keeping her through many trials in her life and allowing her to help others heal.

Completely Yes

BRIANA C. CABELL

Saying yes can be a simple thing. Do you want fries with that? Yes. Mommy, when I grow up can I be a princess? Yes. Would you like a free upgrade to first class? Yes. Would you like some free money? Absolutely YES! But yes, can also be painful, complicated, and frightening.

In many circumstances yes is a contract, a full-on commitment not be entered into lightly. Do you swear to tell the truth, the whole truth, and nothing but the truth? Do you take this man/woman to be your lawfully wedded husband/wife? Do you accept Jesus the Christ, one and only Son of God, as your personal Lord and Savior? Not so easy this time around, is it? Why? There are several levels to the word yes. A yes to the justice system requires complete honesty and lawfulness. A yes to another person requires faithfulness and respect. A yes to God requires all these and more. Total commitment - mind, body, and spirit. Indeed, to walk successfully in excellence we must keep yes on our lips.

Yes, requires us to give up the one thing that many women struggle to hold on to: control. It is our nature to control ourselves and the people and situations around us. Men are indeed the head but women were created to be the neck. Without the neck the head is essentially useless. We want to control our emotions, our children, our careers and even our very essence. But saying yes to God means we must release it all into our Father's hands. In order to display character, wisdom, courage, and strength we must say completely yes!

Just like every other regular person not born in swaddling clothes, I come with a background. It may not be like everyone else's but that is what makes me...me. I could spend many chapters recalling my past. It would take me quite a few strokes to paint you an accurate picture of a complicated life. Indeed, I am no Van Gogh. I would more liken myself to Picasso - on the surface a complicated mess of fallacy but when viewed from a certain angle it creates a priceless work of art. But just as a set of brushes and paints are fairly useless in and of themselves, when they are applied to a blank canvas by a master's hand it becomes a treasure to the world. We are blank canvases, good for little on our own but when skillfully combined with an artist's vision, we are able to captivate the earth.

The Master Artist stepped out into a blank canvas and in His infinite wisdom perceived that it was not good. Using the colorful paints of only His masterful voice He began to call into existence the artwork of the earth. Still, it was not enough. The time had come to call forth the greatest creation a creator can have - a creation that gives continual praise to its creator. A constant reminder of how good that creator is. A timeless representation of a masterstroke. And so, we were created.

You may be wondering what any of this has to do with yes or even becoming a woman of virtue. When the Lord commanded the stars to shine, they said yes. When he called forth the water to separate itself from the heaven, it said yes. When he stepped onto the lifeless dirt and demanded that it become flesh, it said yes. The Creator, however, gave us something he did not give the rest of the earth. He gave us a choice. The fish cannot decide he would like to fly and a dog cannot suddenly lay an egg. When God speaks to the wind it has no option other than to blow. It cannot say no. We, however, can. Time does not permit me to list the ramifications of saying no to God but as we have all said no at one time or another, this is not a foreign concept to us. But what happens when we say yes?

Sandra Crouch expressed the commitment involved in saying yes in her song, Completely Yes. It is a complete and total yielding to the will of the Creator. A simple and powerful song detailing what yes really means. No more I, but it is Christ that lives inside. As newborns we are at the mercy of our parents and other adults and have no option other than to say yes. We are innocent, unwise, and dependent. As we grow and mature our yes gradually develops into no as our desire for independence and experience implores us to find our own way. We have all been there. It is at this crossroads that your answer becomes imperative to your very survival. It is now time to exercise wisdom and put away childish things.

Yes Lord, I will trust you. Yes God, I will believe your word. Yes God, I will follow your commands. Yes Lord, I will put no one else above You. My soul says completely YES. Your character is shaped by your yes. Your wisdom is magnified by your yes. Your courage is tested by your yes. Your strength is fortified by your yes.

Wisdom is defined as knowledge of what is true or right, coupled with just judgment as to action; sagacity, discernment, or insight. How can you gain this insight without saying yes? Wisdom comes from only two sources: time and experience. What greater experience than that of a being that surpasses time itself? Saying yes to

God gives you the benefit of his perfect foresight. When you say yes you give Him permission to make your choices, thus enhancing your life and filling your spiritual cavern with unexplainable peace, joy and love.

Character: the aggregate of features and traits that form the individual nature of some person or thing. What are the traits of a Godless woman? Lowly, weak, frail, empty, desperate, unhappy, lost...these are some of the words that may have come to mind at the thought of being Godless. I honestly feel quite sorrowful when I meet a person of no faith. Where do they hide when the storms of life are raging? Who protects them, guides them, loves them unconditionally? We cannot put that faith in people - the arm of flesh will fail you every time. We cannot trust our money - it cannot purchase anything of real value and holds no value in the emptiness of eternity. You cannot even give all power to the awareness that abides inside the realm of your own capabilities - we are simply empty shells. But when you can say yes to God you are cleansed, refreshed, affirming, hopeful, joyful and capable of giving and receiving love. That becomes your character.

The quality of mind or spirit that enables a person to face difficulty, danger, pain, etc., without fear; bravery—such is the definition of courage. We have not been hindered with the spirit of fear but gifted with Christ who strengthens us. I once saw an Indiana Jones movie in which the title character was on a quest to find the Holy Grail, or the Cup of Life, believed to have been the cup that Jesus Christ used during the Last Supper. It was also used to catch Christ's blood at his crucifixion, after the spear of Longinus pierced his side. The hero was given a book in which all the requirements to reach this sacred object were detailed. In his journey he was tasked to cross a bridge over an unending cavernous hole in which any object would surely be cemented in a vortex of collapsing air falling for an uninterpretable period of time. The challenge is that the bridge was completely invisible, only to show itself in the faith of the terrified Indiana. He had to step out on faith. We have been given a book as well. Often given the acronym of Basic Instructions Before Leaving Earth, it is our written guide to bring us safely over the gaping maw of life which stands ever ready to devour us into its suffocating digestive system with no escape. But stepping out on the faith that comes with our yes gives us an unfailing walkway into the eternity of the Heavenly promise. Even when your human eyes cannot see the path your faith will create it. That, my sisters, is courage.

Gone are the days of the hunter-gatherer wrestling ferocious and toothsome creatures with crudely designed weapons and well-seasoned hands. A physical assent of combat is no longer the measure of true strength. And while physicality will always play a role in our survival, the more pressing definition becomes moral power, firmness, power by reason of influence, authority, resources, or numbers. We have countless historical, biblical and even personal recounts of a Goliath falling to a David, not by David's superior physical prowess but instead relying on ingenuity, cunning, intelligence and faith to be his strength. Women are often weighed down by the moniker of 'the weaker sex.' This is not wholly inaccurate in terms of athleticism, brutish conquering or musculature. However, we must never allow our sex to determine our inner strength. Weakness has the ability to make us stronger than our strongest enemy. When you say yes to God you give your inherent weakness over to Him and in His infinite finality, He uses you as a vessel to pull apart every entangling stronghold imposed upon us. We are like silk—a fine, delicate and beautiful covering that may have no surface perception of security but is actually strong enough to withstand a speeding bullet. Pound-for-pound, silk is stronger than steel. And because of its ability to bend and stretch without breaking, silk is used in parachutes, medical sutures and other life-saving devices. It is that same ability that makes us women of virtue walking in excellence.

Allow me to share my story of yes.

I sat there, my inside man as worn out as a grandmother's old Sunday purse and me outside a broken-down hovel with nary a shred of the happiness that a living space begs for. It was as if I was already dead. In every aspect I was. Separated from my Creator, my heart, like a beautiful crystal vase thrown violently to the floor, was shattered in a million lonely pieces, no longer able to hold anything substantial. My mind was an empty cave of threatening darkness, cold with terror and uncertainty. My breath was as slow and labored as a person being slowly choked by the lifeless stench of cemetery death. With no viable means of escape from my internal prison I closed in on the final chapter of my existence by opening the large bag of assorted pills I had so carefully been saving for this very day. I bathed in the impossibleness of my dingy motel room in stark contrast to sounds of beachgoers only a few hundred feet away: children splashing in the ocean, couples kissing in the sand, merchants selling everything from scripture-emblazoned grains of rice to hermit crabs loping lazily about glass tanks, indifferent to the world around them. The smell of freshly popped and buttered corn, sugar-laden candy treats and deep fried everything wafted for miles but stopped short of my motel room door, unable to penetrate the despairing void lingering on the other side.

Without warning or request a song blared from the impossibly small and dusty screen and reverberated off the tired walls to deep inside my listening senses. The singer sang out loud, "There's a hole in my heart. My soul is bleeding. I need to free my mind and see what I'm feeling. 'Cause Lord knows, Lord knows, I'm tired." How did this stranger, this faceless voice on a recoded movie soundtrack, possibly see through the wires, plastic and electricity to rip my feelings out of my closed throat? Almost robotically I gripped the Ziploc bag that held my fate and waited. There was another sound, this one outside of my cheap dwellings—a church organ. But from where? I stepped onto the creaking balcony and looked toward the heavenly sound.

There was a church next door, which clearly explained the origin of the music but what remained unexplainable was the fact that on a muggy Saturday at dusk, the church was empty. Again, without thought I walked down the stairs toward the sounds with a tear-stained face, bloodshot and swollen eyes, bare feet and a broken spirit. I paid no heed to the curious stares of passersby as I made my way to the doors of the Episcopalian house of worship. The doors - predictably - were locked, the building deserted, and the music now silenced. I stood for a moment staring dumbly at the bolted glass doors. I turned and began to make my way back to my room. When I got there, I became acutely aware of myself and my silence. At that moment it was as if I were emerging from a bout of amnesia in which I couldn't remember who I was but had vivid memories of my pain and no current knowledge of its source. Blinking back hot, dry tears I looked to the Lord—not at the sky, the ceiling, or the floor, but within myself—and said the one word that would change the course of my destiny. I said yes.

Make no mistake in thinking my yes was easy or that immediately the heavens opened up and a burning bush descended and communed with me in a musty hotel room. Do not for a moment believe that from that moment unto this that my life became roses and sunshine and millions in lottery winnings. Far from it. As I have said, yes is not easy. It is not an instantaneous gateway to the promised land. It is a step, a verbal acceptance that is the first step to a lifelong commitment. There will be tears. There will be anger. There will be injustice. There will be pain. However, there will also be victory. It all starts with a yes.

My sisters, we are all here for one purpose, one accord, working toward the same goals: Character, Wisdom, Courage, and Strength. We are creating our paths to being Women of Virtue, Walking in Excellence. A destination cannot be reached without a step. A goal cannot be met without a plan. A war cannot be won without a battle. And we cannot meet our predestination without a yes. Completely yes. My soul says YES!

"For no matter how many promises God has made, they are "Yes" in Christ. And so through him the "Amen" is spoken by us to the glory of God."

(2 Corinthians 1:20, NIV)

Obioma Martin is an inspirational speaker, account-ability-coach, author, small business expert, childcare consultant and esteemed advocate for women's empowerment. Martin's passion for equipping women with the tools they need to, not only survive but, prosper and live audaciously, has launched her into a life of unparalleled servitude, wherein she continues to thrive by helping others.

She is the founder of several organizations that serve the underserved in the community: Obioma Martin, LLC. which provides professional development, mentoring, and coaching to childcare providers and OMART -Women Supporting Women, which supports survivors of domestic abuse and provides opportunities for them to start businesses and return to school.

Martin has helped over 3000 women get off welfare and get the credentials required to complete and further their education. A life-long learner herself, Martin holds multiple degrees; associates degree in Early Childhood Education, bachelors in Childcare Management, a master's degree in Early Childhood Education and Leadership and she is also a Goldman Sachs 10,000 Small Business Program alumni.

Martin is the author of several accountability journals that guide, both men and women, through the process of getting unstuck in every area of their lives. In her latest release, B.R.E.A.T.H.E.- Empowered to Live a Stress-Free Life, Martin shares her stories of hardships, overcoming life's obstacles and the thin line strong women often teeter between superhero and suicide. This gripping composition walks readers through a journey of self-discovery and self-development and brings them out at the end elevated, empowered, and equipped to live their best lives.

Trust the Process

OBIOMA MARTIN

A woman of virtue is a woman of strength, boldness, courage, honesty, and integrity.

She is humble, intelligent, savvy, and resourceful. She is a servant leader and a giver.

Why are these characteristics so important when being a woman of virtue walking in excellence?

At the end of the day all you have is your word. People will forget your name but they will never forget how you treated them. I believe that being a woman of excellence is important because we live in a world where people can be so cold, angry, bitter, and resentful. We have one command as Christians and that is to love God with all our heart and with all our soul and to love our neighbor as ourselves. It takes wisdom, courage and strength to love like Jesus. It takes courage and strength to say, you know what, I don't care if wrong is wrong and everybody is doing it, because right is right even when nobody is doing it. I choose to do right even when wrong is ever present; I choose to go right even when going left is the popular choice.

CHARACTER, WISDOM, COURAGE, AND STRENGTH?

Recall the moments in your life when you had to go through a process and/or processes and maintain your character, wisdom, courage, and strength. What were they? How did you feel? What did you learn? What did you gain? What did you lose?

I'm grateful to share that God is able; God is faithful. I'm so grateful for every lesson.

It was life's lessons, the trials, the triumphs, and the pain from which character, wisdom, courage and strength were developed.

My journey started a long time ago, I was naive, and did not have a clue about what I was being prepared for.

As a teenager, I was always surrounded by wise, mature women. I can remember at the age of 14 being surrounded by three to four women specifically at the church that I had joined. Those women did not know me from Adam, as a young girl in the midst of an identity crisis, looking for love in all the wrong places. I was surrounded by angels. I was surrounded by women who exhibited virtue and strength, honor, tenacity and boldness. I was surrounded by queen mothers and elders.

I was all caught up in being caught up as an adolescent. I can remember trying to fit in and trying to be accepted, wanting to be accepted, wanting to be validated. I can remember being in circles that I knew I shouldn't have been in. I can remember going to places that I knew I didn't fit in, but because I was going through an identity crisis, I wanted to be wherever I thought I would be accepted. And sometimes those places and those people did not always do right by me, did not always serve me well. But it was through those struggles an identity crisis, not quite knowing who I was or whose I was, that my character began to take form.

There was a boldness that began to develop on the inside of me that I did not know was there. As I journeyed through adolescence, I can remember becoming pregnant at the age of 16 and being devastated.

I was on my way to becoming someone great. I can remember being ashamed and being embarrassed. It was during those early years as a teen mom that I began to understand that even though I had made this mistake, even though I had had sex out of wedlock, even though the father of my child had no interest in being a father, I knew that there was more. I knew that there was a promise. I knew that there was a hope. I knew that this pregnancy was not going to change my destiny. I did not understand how truly lost I was. I was broken; I felt all alone. I did not feel love; I did not feel like life was worth living, even though there was a glimmer of hope, even though on the inside of me I knew that there was more. There was more; there was a promise.

As I think back over my life, God was working all things together for my good even in my pain. There was purpose.

And so, I continue my journey.

As a young single mom and even now looking back, I'm so grateful that my mom, in the midst of our dysfunction, had a standard for my life. Even when I thought the standard was no longer there, even though the lines appeared to be blurred and their color appeared often to be fading, there was a standard. My mom said,

"Even though you are now a teen mom, you will graduate on time, with honors. You will not be a dropout. You will finish school; you will be somebody; you are somebody." That was her stand.

My mom spoke life into me and into my situation. She spoke life to those blurred lines, and she refused to allow my mistake or my pain to dictate my purpose. And for that, I'm forever grateful.

My mother saw potential. My mother saw me as a winner, even when I did not see myself as a winner.

I am a woman of excellence. I am a woman of integrity and virtue because of the standard that was set before me—the bar that was raised. I know I can walk with my head lifted high, being a woman of high regard, a woman who refuses to allow those lines to be blurred again, because I now know who I am and whose I am.

I continue to press toward the mark of the high calling. I continue to be as that Proverbs 31 woman was described. I continue to be everything that my God has called me to be, not because I'm perfect, 'cause I'm flawed. But because I know that abundance is my birthright. I know that greatness is my destiny.

I know that even though I was birthed in sin and shaped in iniquity, I know the plans that God has for me. And it's a future full of possibility.

I know that I am enough. I am enough, because God made me enough.

You will experience situations in the workplace and your family, and your relationships where everything on the inside of you, everything that you want and believe, is challenged. People will test you; people continue to test me. I work with women of all ages, young and old, who come from various socio-economic backgrounds, from trauma and dysfunction. I work with women who are hurt, and broken down and in prison in their minds, so because they are coming from a place of brokenness, they hurt people.

Every single day I have to make a decision to be better. I have to make a decision to be the change that I seek to be, the change that I want to be. I have to make a decision that in spite of the hurt, in spite of the lies, in spite of the deceit, in spite of the narrative, I will rise, and that I'll be the bigger person.

I know what it's like to love and not to be loved back. I know what it's like to give your all to a project and to a person, to a sister, and your kindness and your compassion is used against you. I know what it's like to be in unhealthy, toxic relationships with both men and women. I know what it's like to serve in ministry and be empty and to feel depleted.

I can say to you today with full assurance that it is because of those things and those experiences, I am a woman who now walks in virtue and in victory and in excellence. I refuse to be a statistic. I refuse to allow my past to dictate my future. I allow every lesson to sharpen me to make me better. I allow what the enemy attempts to do to distract me to drive me to my destiny.

I rise up every day with a heart of praise and a posture of Thanksgiving, because I'm grateful. I'm grateful that the fire did not burn me.

I recently endured a situation with a young lady who gave me this very sad story about how she and her mom were being put out by a sheriff. Her stepfather, her mom's husband, had deserted them and didn't pay the bills. I don't know why I believed this story but I did and I remember a couple of people at the school where I teach saying, "Miss O, don't get involved; don't believe it" and even though I was warned not to I told this young lady I had an empty house. I said, "You know I'm going to help you. I'm not going allow you to be homeless. I'm not gonna see you out on the street" and so I decided to help her against wise counsel and she moved in and I didn't charge them for the first month.

Now when January came the young lady started asking whether I had a renter's license and I said no, I only had a business license and was planning to turn the house into a faith house for women with children and teen parents. She said that her uncle said I needed a license. Eventually her mom moved in a boyfriend then she moved in her son with his girlfriend and I asked them to leave because the house was supposed to just be for the young lady and her mom. They did not leave and it took me eight months to get them out of my house. I had to go through the sheriff's department in my county to have them removed.

Throughout this process I was very nice and remained compassionate. I was not bitter or angry at this point; I just wanted them out of my house. When I would go to my house to check on them, they got very mean and nasty and really destroyed the house and just didn't take care of it and the house began go downhill. Even when we showed up in court both the young lady and her mom created a narrative that just was not true, saying that I was harassing them and others came into the house and I gave them notice and I was watching them from a camera, and I didn't even have any cameras in the house. Any time I coming to the house I let them know, so in that moment I was really feeling overwhelmed that I was even in this situation. Here I was just trying to help and my kindness and compassion were now being turned against me and so I just began to pray. I began to pray and really seek the Lord in this situation because at the end of the day I wanted to be the change, I wanted to be different and in spite of how badly they were treating me and the lies that they were telling about me, I knew that I had a commitment to love them like they were still my neighbor.

My intentions were to help and I was committed to helping and so even when I saw the young lady at school I would say to her, "You know this isn't right; why are you doing this?" and she said, "Well, that's my mom and I'm not going to choose you over my mom. I'm going to side with my mom." It really hurt me to my core and so I had to make a decision to go because at the end of the day I felt like I was doing all I felt I had left to do, which was to help. I can't control somebody else's motive or agenda. I can't control what people do or say but I can take responsibility for my actions and I can control my emotions toward their reactions. I did not retaliate. At the end of the day everything was turned in my favor and the sheriff told them that they had 45 days to leave the property. I won because in spite of the adversities and opposition, I did right and justice prevailed, love prevailed. So when I think about my journey of having to have character, wisdom and strength and walk in excellence, I still did right by that young lady and I continue to do right by other young ladies in similar situations.

It is my hope that those who read this chapter this book will be empowered to boldly take a stand against injustice, against the things that are wrong in their community, in their home, in their relationships—to say I am enough and I don't have to settle and I don't have to go below. I can take the high road. I can be the change; I can be the difference. I don't have to do what everybody else is doing. I don't have to be who everybody else says that they want me to be. I can make a decision to be who God created me to be.

It is my prayer that as women read this chapter, they will be encouraged to just maintain their standards and to advocate for other people, but often, when it comes to us, we have a double standard. We sometimes think, *Oh no, I'm OK. I know I'm not good enough for there; I can't eat there; oh, that's too expensive; oh, I'm gonna get them back, oh, I'm going to treat them the way they treated me.* I'm saying to you today, every woman who is reading this chapter, no more double standards. You are enough. You are a woman of virtue. You are a woman of excellence. Don't allow your past to define you or dictate your future. You are enough because when God created you before the foundation of the Earth, he created you enough.

Best-selling author, teacher, consultant, orator, and philanthropist Charlene Day of KeLabe provides her expertise in business networking, collaboration, and partnerships to develop your business aspirations. You can read about her history and current efforts in imparting wisdom and strategy for life and business. It shows the depths of her knowledge and experience, along with a profound appreciation for the considerable hurdles that we all must overcome to be our best. Through events, classes, books, and coaching from Washington, DC to an international scale, Charlene has reached countless masses of professionals young and old. Her purpose is bringing people together to find and create opportunities to function in their possibilities.

Charlene received her Bachelors of Science Degree in Journalism & Mass Communication - P.R. M.S. in Education and Communication from North Carolina A&T. She pursued post graduate works at Duke University in Technical Communication and Study Aboard at Oxford with focused studies in Communications on CS Lewis.

Walk It Out

CHARLENE DAY

I was in my mother's womb when she fell in the tub of hot water. It was a month before my arrival. She began panicking. Suddenly, her panic turned into a prayer and prayer turned into praise. She was rushed to the hospital, praying for my survival. "By faith," she said, "I believed that you would be all right. I had already experienced God's miracles. By God's assurance of His spirit, I was comforted and you began to settle." She said, "I didn't get my strength from those doctors and nurses. All of my help came from the Lord."

Every time she tells me this story, I hear how life situations have made her into the woman she is today. They have shaped her character, given her wisdom to pass along to me, made her courageous in the eyes of defeat and strengthened her in time of weakness. All of this has been a big contribution to how I became a woman of virtue walking in excellence.

I draw so much strength from this story. I understand that life is our teacher and provides us with lessons to apply to every test. With some of those lessons our pain brings forth glory. I also understand that there must be a building of our character and a process associated with that pain to get us to excellence.

The word of God clearly states:

"Therefore, since we have been justified through faith, we have peace with God through our Lord Jesus Christ, through whom we have gained access by faith into this grace in which we stand; and we rejoice in the hope of the glory of God. Not only so, but we also glory in our sufferings, because we know that suffering produces perseverance; perseverance, character; and character, hope. And hope does not put us to shame, because God's love has been poured out into our hearts through the Holy Spirit, who has been given to us." (Romans 5:1-5, NIV).

Defining a woman of virtue is to describe women like my mom, who have influenced my life. They are women who can stand in their power after their failures and regain their strength by using it to empower others.

Moreover, in this chapter, you will see me recall moments in my life when I had to go through a process of maintaining my character because I used the wisdom of my experience. You'll journey with me to visualize me gleaning my wisdom from others' trials and errors, for these are the people who impacted and influenced my life decisions. You'll walk with me to watch me courageously speak up and stand up for what's right. Last, you'll dance with me as I regain my strength to walk out all my decisions in excellence. All in all, you will gain nine lessons that have guided me to be the best version of me as a woman of virtue walking in excellence: Enjoy Waiting, Paying Attention, Listening, Becoming Knowledgeable, Being Intentional, Timing, Organizing, Understanding, and Trust.

In order to overcome anything in life you must apply the lessons taught from the past.

WAITING IS MANDATORY

Walter and his wife were longtime friends of mine. Walter had always been known as being strict. Get it done or get out of his way. In other words, he wasn't very patient with his employees nor with himself. He hated waiting on anything, including fast food in a drive-through. Life would change for Walter when his wife was diagnosed with a debilitating disease that took her eyesight. I watched his lifestyle change from losing his job to working as a waiter to make ends meet for him and his family. For years, I watched his resistance at taking on this responsibility. Finally, he got it. He told me that life has a funny way of getting you to be what God needs you to be for yourself. He said for years he prayed for patience and when God allowed this to come upon his family, he hated God for it. "Now, Charlene, I get it." By watching his circumstances take place right before my eyes, I too got it. I understood that God wants us to practice patience daily in everything that we do.

Lesson: You walk it out by learning to wait. Practice patience and kindness. Be patient. If not, God will always create lessons to teach you how to be patient.

PAY ATTENTION

Athena, also referred to as Athene, is a very important goddess of many things. She is goddess of wisdom, courage, inspiration, civilization, law and justice, strategic warfare, mathematics, strength, strategy, the arts, crafts, and skill. She is known most specifically for her strategic skill in warfare and is often portrayed as companion of heroes and is the patron goddess of heroic endeavors.

Understanding the goddess Athena's gifts helps me to seek excellence, pay attention to life lessons, learn from them and apply them as much as possible. This helps me be more strategic in my alliances with people.

Lesson: Pay attention to things around you. It will help you think and become strategic.

LISTENING WINS WARS

There are several times my family has asked me why I watch war stories. "Why do you like the History Channel? It's so boring." I chuckle. It can be quite daunting to watch and listen if you think the mundane commentary is causing you to fall asleep.

However, there are points I would like to help you to appreciate. In World War II, in 1945, we dropped the bomb on Japan. I wasn't born but it was my birthday month. I often wonder how they knew. How did they win the war when we were so close to losing? There were specialized, skilled military units that were able to provide information to move with accuracy and speed. Long story short... they listened. They decoded. Such has been my life. I have used my skills in listening to hear what I need to overcome any situation.

Lesson: Listening is a practiced skill. Practicing it daily will help you hear things that're needed to overcome life's most challenging battles.

WHEN APPLIED, KNOWLEDGE IS POWERFUL

Commonly, there are experiences that will lead you to believe that you have learned nothing but hurt, pain and shame. Despite it all, look at the experience as an opportunity to gain knowledge. See yourself as an instrument of the Almighty to use what you have learned to apply in your life should the situation happen again. Remember, knowledge prevents us from making the same mistakes we made in the past. According to an article in *Psychology Today* (Henriques, 2011), knowledge is psychology. It is referred to as the application of the knowledge, which can be used to understand events, treat mental health issues, and improve education, employment, and relationships. Use your knowledge to become more powerful in your purpose.

Lesson: Use your knowledge to understand your purpose.

BE INTENTIONAL

Being intentional is doing everything on purpose, on a specific date, time and place. Using a calendar is my number one tool. Using kindness is right next to it. It is my tool to break the bad energy to make a powerful impact.

I am always taken aback by people who just think doing things without a plan works. It doesn't. I believe the old saying, "If you fail to plan you plan to fail." In 2010, I was in my last year in graduate school. One of my professors was challenging my gifting of kindness. One of my strong talents is connections and collaborations. With this comes the power to negotiate and get almost anything I want. A fellow student had not done her due diligence to find her own site. The professor had taken upon herself to give the young lady my lead on an internship, in which I had established the relationship. It was not a pretty picture. I had totally no respect for her. I had worked hard to pursue this position. I went to talk to my advisor and told her what had happened. I also talked to my graduate mentor. The solution was let it go and let her show her hand. I did just that. Months later we had to present about our internship site. We were to talk about our experience and what our plans were after graduation. That night I did only what I was asked. Intentionally, after graduation I had set a meeting up with my advisor and the professor to let her know that if she ever needed me for anything, I would be glad to assist her in helping to get internships. I told her I was pretty good at getting in the door of any corporation I needed to make the deal happen. She glared with a thank you. I smiled with purpose. I think you have to be just as intentional about knowing where you are going as you do with what you are doing. My intention was to leave an impact on the school for other students and faculty that came behind me.

Lesson: Be intentional about every aspect of your life to perform at your highest and best self.

TIME IS OF THE ESSENCE

Time is a precious commodity to me. It is the pure essence of life. To walk in excellence is to value your time and the time of others. It is the flower you want to smell every day when you awaken. You learn to appreciate it once you have lost it through health, life, difficult circumstances, and financial downturn. Of course, there are others to name. However, I would sum it up to say that time waits for no one, so use it wisely. It harms no one. It is there to serve its purpose timely.

Lesson: Value time

LIFE IS EASIER WHEN ORGANIZED

Do you want to really be a show-off? Do you really want people to say you do things in excellency? Start organizing every area of your life. It has saved my life and made it easier. Simple things such as emptying my closet, selling everything, throwing away old files, and writing out my day the night before have been ways I've organized to make life easier. The best part of my getting organized is that I landed a contract because I was able to complete the proposal that I had written months ahead of time. Get organized and watch your life flourish.

Lesson: Getting organized will make your life easier.

EVERY STUDENT NEEDS UNDERSTANDING

Eunice was an older lady who taught me the simple lessons of understanding. She told me how she got this character trait through her own mom. She seemed to be very forgiving and got that people are people. They need guidance. The problem is them not seeking it. I value that in her. I also value that getting understanding is bringing those around you who have what you need or support you on your journey to getting what you need. For example, coaches and professional and girlfriend networks are things to help me to build my confidence and walk in excellence in my purpose.

Lesson: Hire and surround yourself with people who understand what you need.

TRUST WILL TRANSFORM YOUR LIFE

Trust is assured reliance on the character, ability, or truth of someone or something. Transforming is to make a thorough or dramatic change in the form, appearance or character or condition. Both are processes that we must go through to see change in our life. I truly believe that whatever you are called to do, it will happen only by going through the process and trusting it. The best way that I finally received this for myself was hearing this statement: "Whatever the vision, there is provision; trust that."

Lesson: Trust the process. It will transform your life.

As you can see through the narrative writings shared with each key principle, my excellence came from the lessons of my failure. I have learned that you cannot be excellent at anything without being a failure at something. Life was and is my teacher. The lessons I learned from the teacher are to be studied, tested, practiced and applied. Today, I can stand in character, wisdom, courage, and strength, due to the fact that I have been tested, practiced each day until I got better, and applied the principles to every aspect of my life. As you continue to walk in virtue and demonstrate excellence, take each life lesson, learn from it, adjust, and change. Change to become the woman you were called and created to be. Becoming the best version of you is the greatest accomplishment that you will ever do for yourself and others.

Reference
Henriques, Gregg. (2011). Psychology Defined. What, exactly, is psychology? *Psychology Today.*

··

*"And let us not be weary
in well doing: for in due
season we shall reap,
if we faint not."*

(Galatians 6:9, KJV)

··

Tela C. Jones was born and raised in Bremerton Washington in June, 1959 and is 60 years old. She is the third oldest of eight children. Tela is a 40-year cancer survivor, having been diagnosed when she was just 20 years old.

Ms. Jones earned her B.A from The Evergreen State College Tacoma WA., in 2000, the first one in her family to achieve this milestone. She went on to Earn her M.A. Ed. In 2005 from Antioch University Seattle. Tela earned her master's certificate in Human Resource management in 2015, from Trident University. She has worked in the Social Services field for over 30 years. She has a strong professional background working with the special need's population.

Tela has worked with the Department of Defense for 11 years, she is currently employed with Fairfax County Department of Family services.

She currently resides in Southern MD.

After the Weeping, Then What?

TELA C. JONES

Psalms 30:5, NKJV "Weeping may endure for a night but joy cometh in the morning." This was once the only scripture I lived by and leaned on in my early Christian walk. After all, this scripture has brought me through many tough days.

I was born and raised in Bremerton, Washington, a small navy town about an hour and fifteen-minute drive west of Seattle. I have lasting and impactful memories of my infant and elementary years. I am the third oldest of eight children. I spent a lot of time from ages one and two with my godmother Ms. Lula Holland. My godfather Ulysses Holland was a Pentecostal minister and we spent lots of time in church as a family. I was raised by my maternal aunt, Daisy Robinson, for most of my infant and elementary years, until the age of 10. She lived in Tacoma, WA, and then Seattle. Aunt Daisy's husband Stanley Robinson was a Baptist preacher. My early childhood was covered in prayers and love. I have memories of traveling by car to Detroit, Michigan for vacation with them. My purpose seemed to have been chosen for me early in my life.

I have fond memories of living with my aunt and my cousins. I remember Sunday mornings being dressed up for church. I always had a pretty dress and white gloves on and my hair was perfect. My offering for church was always tied in a white hanky with little pink and yellow flowers stitched on it and tied in a small knot. I sat on the front row with my aunt during services, often fidgeting. I had the best life ever. Christmas was always my aunt's favorite season; that's when the house was decorated festively and the whole Thomas family would come and stay a couple of days, share and enjoy the holiday. I remember the big house with the long wood banister that served as a slide for me on many days.

Suddenly, as if the pages of my life turned, everything that I once grew to love and cherish as a child seemed to vanish. My aunt passed away when I was 10 years old. As a child I didn't understand what was happening in my life. All I knew is that my heart was torn apart and tears would be my voice. After my aunt's death I returned to my mother's home. By then she had remarried and my new stepfather had asked that me and my younger brother Sam come back home to be a family. Sam spent a lot of time with my other aunt, Jeanni, as I did with Aunt Daisy.

I went from having my own room to sharing a room with my two other sisters. I felt very cramped and closed in. I felt as if I really did not know them at all. Sometimes I felt like an outsider. I adjusted as well as I could and remained quiet and to myself. I was most likely depressed as a child but didn't know it. How ironic that my childhood would come into play as I became an adult and worked with children in foster care. Somehow, I could relate to their grief and loss of family, only in a different way. I had another home to go to with family right away. Many of the children I provide services for have lost their connections to their birth families.

Our family moved to the suburbs. I soon found myself away from my cousins and living in an area where people didn't look like me. I remember going to fifth grade and the only children of color were me and my brothers and two other children. My teen years were interesting. In junior high, I was a cheerleader and one of the first African Americans to be voted a cheerleader in the school's history. I think you get a sense of the environment I was educated in. I ran track, played basketball and played tennis for fun.

High school was more of a challenge for me, not academically but socially. I had a couple of best friends whom I still remain in contact with, Bonita and Jeannette. I valued their friendships then and now. Both ladies are Caucasian, and they were friends with me when it was not popular to hang with African Americans. Those two made me feel like any other teenager and accepted me for who I was.

I married at 18 and had my first child in that same year, 1978. I met my children's father in my senior year and just knew I would have the life of a little yellow house with a picket fence and would live happily ever after. I had joined a Pentecostal church and loved the fellowship I had there. My husband did not join, nor did he attend church. I studied the Bible and held it close to my heart; after all, as a child I learned the word of God early on and it was embedded in my spirit. After my second daughter was born things went downhill in my marriage. What I thought was a perfect life was not. News flash: my life became a living hell. I had never experienced domestic violence. It was introduced to my life and was foreign to me. I was not raised around violence and it was tearing me apart. I confided in my pastor for counsel, but that did not stop the violence. My scripture day in and day out was Psalm 30; with tears many nights I stayed on my knees before the Lord, only being able to moan and cry and ask for his help. After all, I did know how to pray. I remember when my daughters were one and two their father came home drunk and became violent, the worst I had seen from him. I remember fighting back and fearing death at the same time. Somehow, I found the courage and strength to fight. I realized that I was holding my daughter in my arms and my husband was fighting me. Something triggered inside me (most likely my motherly instinct) and at that very moment I realized that either I was going to die, or he was. My children deserved better and I was the only one who could make that happen. God blessed me to have the courage and the strength and the mind to leave and not look back.

The next six months after I left my husband, it seemed like my life was compounded with more disappointment. I moved my girls and myself to our own apartment after staying with friends. I was not used to standing in welfare lines and asking for help. My mother would always say, "I have never had a day on welfare. I raised all eight of you while working hard." I felt ashamed and embarrassed. To make things worse, I was diagnosed with stage 3 cancer and all I could do was cry. I saw my future flash before me. Prayers and tears day and night were my routine forever, it seemed.

Joy finally came in the morning! After many doctor appointments and prayers and fasting and surgery, I was cancer free a year later. I gained strength through the word of God daily and courage to fight on. I even became a volunteer for the local shelter for battered women. I would become an advocate and give counsel and comfort to those who could not help or speak for themselves. I saw and learned many things through serving and helping others, and it felt good to give back.

God would continue to work in my life and use me to uplift, edify and comfort other women. I loved to volunteer my time. I went back and volunteered and gave back to the food banks I once frequented. I was blessed with a great job working for the state of Washington and moved on and up with the state for 22 years. I attended college in Tacoma and graduated with my Bachelor's degree in 2000. It was one of my greatest achievements. I was the first in my family to do so at that time, out of five generations. I later went on to complete my Master's in education in 2005, with much encouragement from my pastor, Dr. Joel Odimba. I later completed my Master's certificate in Human Resources in 2014 from Trident University.

After the weeping I have learned how to go on and how to not lean on what I see with my eyes but what I see in my spirit and what I see in the word. I have taken life's stings and rubbed them with the salve of God's lessons and learned from each experience. I am so grateful to be alive.

My testimony has not been that I have been saved all my life. My testimony is that I have come through many adversities in my life and I have overcome many obstacles, heartaches, heartbreaks, disappointments, losses, and failed attempts at love. But what I have gained throughout this process called life is that I am strong, I am resilient, I am determined, I am an up-lifter and an encourager, and a fighter for justice and equality. I never knew I could fight until I had to. I did not know that I could encourage anyone after going through so much in my life and feeling so broken. Out of brokenness I emerged a powerful, God-fearing vessel of honor. I praise God he gave me a heart to love, serve and be obedient to His word. I stand firm in my commitment to give back and speak up and lift my sisters who may need an encouraging word or an outstretched hand or a just a smile.

I have great love and respect and admiration for the women who bore, raised, molded, encouraged and prayed for me. "For by thee I have run through a troop and by my god have I leaped over a wall" (Psalms 18:29, KJV). Many days I turned my face to the wall as Hezekiah did in Jerimiah 38:2. There were many instances where I felt that I had wrestled with the angel as Jacob did and refused to give up until the Lord blessed me.

Today I live unapologetically. I will never be a slave to my past. It was a stepping stone to a higher me. I have never chased blessings; I chased the One who could give the blessings. I praise God that I found safety in the process of him changing me and my life; after all, he has unleashed my limitless potential. Don't ever give up or give in; be a blessing to others and your life will be blessed. Just think, if you have your hands full of wisdom, life, words, encouragement, gifts (natural and spiritual), and kindness you are holding onto and not sharing with others, you can't get a blessing in your hands; if they are full already nothing new can come in. Release those blessings to others and you will be amazed at how much more your life is blessed, fulfilled and purposeful.

I am in no way perfect, nor has my life been. I had to learn how to ignore the distractions and limit the negativity of the world. I praise God he led me to a ministry and a pastor who saw the gifts God placed in me, and he allowed me to walk in those gifts. This man has been a mentor, an encourager, a confidence builder, and a believer in my purpose and I thank God for Dr. Joel Odimba Pastor of my home church, First Love International.

Today my husband and I currently volunteer for American Disabled Veterans. I enjoy Relay for Life every year as a 39-year cancer survivor and an encourager for others fighting this battle. I am a huge Washington Redskins fan.

This is only a glimpse of the blessed life God has given me. There is much more to my story.

Blessings to you all.

Gina S. Duncan is the CEO and Owner of the Gina S. Duncan Insurance Agency. She was born and raised in Paterson, NJ. She began her career working for the Passaic County Board of Social Services as a Clerk Typist and later as a Data Analyst at Kearfott Guidance and Navigation Corporation.

In 1995, Gina landed a job at State Farm Insurance Company. While employed with State Farm, she quickly rose through the ranks, being promoted to the highest of every position she held. In 1995, she also became a Certified Tax Preparer for H&R Block and later opened her own tax preparation business.

Gina received her Bachelor of Arts Degree in Communications in May 2001. After graduation and in search of a better life for her children, she transferred with State Farm Insurance Company to work in their Frederick, Maryland operations center. She lived in Frederick for one year and in 2002, she moved to Charles Town, WV and lived there for seven years. In 2005, Gina received her Maryland Real Estate License and in 2006 she received her

West Virginia Real Estate License. In 2009, she received another promotion with State Farm Insurance Company and moved back to Maryland.

After working for State Farm for 24 years and becoming an insurance matter expert, Gina decided to take the leap of faith to start her own company. The Gina S. Duncan Insurance Agency is now located in Upper Marlboro, MD.

Gina is licensed in seven states MD, VA, FL, NC, WV, DE and NJ (her home state). She is also a certified Notary Republic and is a member of the Sisters 4 Sisters Network Inc., where she holds office as Membership Director. She is a committee member of the Maryland Black Chamber of Commerce and was the first member to join the new Bi-County Business Roundtable. She is also a member of the Beech Tree Community Communications Committee.

Gina is married to Robert Duncan III. They have four children: A'Shanti Bowman, A'Jahni Bowman, Robert Duncan IV and Cheyenne Duncan. Gina loves her family and friends and is looking forward to what God has pre-destined for her.

A Spoken Word

GINA S. DUNCAN

It all started from a spoken word. My Mom was an identical twin she died when I was three, I could not remember her, as hard as I tried. My dad died when I was seven, at least this is who I thought was my dad, but when I was fifteen, I found out he wasn't biological dad, but he was the only man I called my father and dad. My life thus far has consisted of revelations, hard work and miracles which has made me into the person I am today. I know everyone says this, but it's true. We all have a destiny and a purpose, my purpose is to show, love, kindness and support those who are less fortunate than myself. I was born in Paterson, New Jersey the youngest of four children to Alphonso and Florene Roper. It all started when my Mom died, what does a three-year-old know? When I was in between m my teens and adult years when I realized I could never visit my Mom's gravesite. Why? Because Mom died without insurance to bury her, having left a husband and four children with nothing. My dad was a drug attic, so you know he was thinking about insurance. I spoke a word, "when I get older, I will never leave my family to fend for themselves, the way our parents left us". Not knowing what my destiny would be, I spoke it. After my Dad was killed (stabbed to death), my Grandmother and Grandfather, John and Reba Harris, raised us as their own. Four children, me three, my sister seven, my brother eight and my older brother fourteen. My Grandparents were already in their early fifties, they didn't ask for this responsibility, but it was upon them. They provided us with a good life we grew up to respect our elders, say hello, thank you, please, good morning, good night and God Bless you. My Grandmother was my role model, I loved her more than words can ever express here on paper. She taught me everything I know with her 4th grade education. She inspired me to own my own property, maintain and keep property, to do finances (balance a check book), open a savings account, use a Christmas club to your advantage, cook, act like a lady, have manners, decorate and keep house, plant a garden, landscape and most of all she taught us all about God and our Lord and savior Jesus Christ. I was in church every Sunday, in every church play, on the choir, singing and praising God for keeping me. My biggest desire as a child was to have a family of my own and be a wife one day. This was the first test of my faith, when I a teenager, I became pregnant. I was scared and afraid. I kept it to myself, but we know whatever's done in the dark will come to light. I started to get sick, really sick, at times I could not walk. I chose to stay in my room and sleep instead of telling someone. My boyfriend at the time, kept saying you are not well, we need to take you to the hospital, he carried me from my bed into the car and into the emergency room. I had an ectopic pregnancy and could've died. The doctor who performed my surgery said I would not have lived past that night if I did not come in. But God's salvation through the doctor said since I was so young, he was not able to save my left ovary and fallopian tube but saved the right side so that I could conceive when I was older. It left me with an ugly scar on my stomach (that I'm still embarrassed about today) but I was happy I would be able to have children one day. God performed his first miracle in life. Praise God.

I finished high school with good grades. After graduation I approached my Grandmother to tell her I wanted to go to college, she said they couldn't afford to send me. I thought to myself If I wanted things out of life, I would work and send myself to college. I was 18 years old when I landed a job as a Clerk Typist at the Passaic County Board of Social Services in the town I lived. I would walk several miles to and from work or take the bus. I soon realized one of my neighbors a friend of my brothers worked thereto. I begin to ride share with her. I would wait walk to her home a few doors down and wait for her to leave. She was always late, which in turn made me late. I loved that job, I did well at it, I was noticed by my boss as a conscientious worker. He recommended me for a promotion after a year. I was promoted to the fiscal department, where my responsibilities grew. I bought my first car it was a brand new 1997 Mitsubishi mirage, I was so proud of myself. I had a car and insurance payment as well as rent that I would pay my grandmother as well as incidentals. I realized I needed to make more money. I applied for a position with Kearfott Guidance and Navigation Corporation, an Aerospace company which I knew nothing about. They hired me as a Data Analyst, trained me for the position. I worked under a woman who was a stickler for perfection, and structure. She was well respected in the company; this was good for me as I could learn from her. I watched her like a hawk, studying her well spoken words and mimicking her work ethics; I followed her every move, and became better each day under her. I was soon promoted to a Sr. Data Analyst, meeting with personnel from Lockheed Martin and Grumman. I worked on huge aerospace contracts, gave presentations. I loved my job, I worked here for seven years. During the years of working at Kearfott, my adult life started to begin. My grandmother got sick, it was not a long illness, and it didn't matter if it was. I hung in there with her, would visit her every day in the hospital, when she came home my sister and I took care of her. My grandmother passed in 1988, I was 21 years old. My grandfather passed two years later, in the home we lived in. My oldest brother found him dead in his bed. I was 23, grandpa died from a combination of diabetes and a broken heart; my grandparents were married for over 40 years. There we were again; my brothers and sister and I were alone. At least this time I was able to take care of myself, my grandparents also left us proceeds from their life insurance policies (they didn't want us to ever struggle again). This was profound because it was what I spoke when I was young. It was my grand-mothers wish she say tome "I pray God would allow me to live to see you get grown". God kept his promise to her. I was young and alone, I met my boyfriend at my Grandmother's funeral. He was a friend of my brothers. We dated for three years, before I became pregnant with my son. I longed for a family since the matriarch and patriarch were no longer around. I became pregnant and gave birth to my first born A'Shanti Bowman in 1991, I was as happy as anyone could be. I had someone to call my own, a child a longed for, a family that I could cherish for life. My eldest brother passed in 1994. I experienced so much tragedy, but I didn't let anything stop me from my faith. I was a young adult with a home, that my grandparents left me, a child and a boyfriend. I had my Aunt Clory my Mothers Identical twin sister. She was there for us like she was our mother. She played a major role in our lives before and after the passing of my grandmother and grandfather. But God has a way of working things out, everything happens in due season. My biological grandmother came into my life, after the passing of my Grandmother. It was like God gave me a new beginning, he blessed me with additional family members I had not known. With all this, I landed a job at State Farm Insurance company in 1995. I was now a Mom and had to make a way for my family. My boyfriend and I got married in 1997 and welcomed another child into the world A'Jahni Bowman in 1998. While at State Farm I landed several promotions but couldn't go any farther in my career unless I had a Degree. I studied for my Degree, it took me ten years and two children later, but I did it. Being driven I also went to school to become a certified tax preparer. I worked for H&R Block for two years before opening up my own Business called Bowman Tax Enterprise. I did this on the side while working full time. I enjoyed being an entrepreneur and decided I would leave my job at State Farm one day to do so. While still working for the company, and after graduating College. We relocated to Maryland so that our children would have a better chance at life. I decided I would get my Real Estate License. I got my Real Estate License in Maryland, and after moving to West Virginia to purchase our first purchased home together as a married couple. We decided to get our home built from the ground up. I also obtained my Real Estate License in West Virginia. I started selling Real Estate and did particularly well, I did so well I decided I would leave my full-time gig. That's when things with south and the Real Estate market crashed. It was bitter sweet, as I still had my job but so desperately wanted to leave but was unable to. I stayed with State Farm and prayed for another opportunity to come. All during my career with State Farm God was preparing me to leave, however I was fearful. God promised I would have my own business one day that I desired. I just couldn't see how. In 2013 due to marital problems, addiction and abuse, I separated from my husband. I moved out of our home my second home, built from the ground up. It was my dream home. My youngest child remained with me and my eldest stayed with his dad. My eldest was already in his last two years of college, so that made since. During the separation I struggled to make ends meet, I lived paycheck to paycheck. I kept the faith, I went to church every Sunday, paid my tithes and didn't give up on my family or my dream. My husband at the time tried to destroy me. He did everything in his power to break me, he destroyed my credit, would spy on me and slandered my name. I ended up claiming bankruptcy to stay afloat and filed for divorce. While single God saw to it that I became busy at work, so busy that I would work a lot of overtime. I was also able to work from home and start a savings account. While working I would help customers like they were my family members. I would get great reviews from my managers and awesome customer service letters. I would send referrals to two Agents in particular. It was still in the back of my mind, that I wanted to be an Agent one day. To help others and teach others what I knew about insurance and how it could help them. After my divorce, claiming bankruptcy and receiving another rent increase notice, I spoke that I was going to buy a home because I was tired of paying rent. I had the audacity to apply for a mortgage loan. What was I thinking, I had just declared bankruptcy, it had not been a year? But that's what God told me to do, so I listened. Where had this thought come from. It was just me, no one to fall back on, but I did muster up a small savings. After applying for the mortgage, several weeks went by without a word. I called the loan officer to see what was going on. She told me that my loan documents would need to be sent to the credit committee. Then God spoke again and told me to write a letter to the company. I listened to God and wrote a letter. Meanwhile time was going by, but my savings account was going up as well as my credit score (right after bankruptcy). Afterwards I wrote another letter to God and put it in my bible. I asked God to allow my loan to be approved, with no down payment and no closing cost. (I keep these letters in my bible if anyone is interested in seeing them). Several weeks later the loan officer called to advise this has never happened, but my loan had been approved. God performed a miracle for me! I was thankful and grateful. I praised his holy name. The mortgage amount wasn't for much, but it was approved. It took me awhile to find a home, I started looking for foreclosures, because that's all I thought I could get. But all the foreclosures I looked at needed too many repairs and were not in the area I desired to live in. I did find a nice town home that needed little work. I put a contract on it, and it was accepted. I was a home owner again. While looking for my home, three years after my separation and my recent divorce, I met a nice man. He was the best man I had ever had. He was kind, considerate, respectful and nice looking, needless to say it was love at first sight and we never parted since our first date. We got married 14 months later. Most people thought it was too soon, but when you know what you want, why wait? After our marriage, my youngest A'Jahni and his eldest Robert lived with us. My eldest son came to live with us too. My daughter would come up for holidays and summer vacations. We needed a bigger home. We started looking for another home, but as we know everything in the DMV is pricey. One day while looking God spoke to me again, he said clearly, "Why are you looking for what you already have"? I didn't understand at first, but it dawned on me that I still owned the home that I gracefully walked away from. The home my ex was renting out making a profit. The one he lived in with his girlfriend. I contacted my Ex to tell him I received a letter in the mail that the home was going to foreclosure. I explained instead of letting it go to foreclosure we were interested in buying him out. He openly agreed but secretly he had no intentions on giving up the home. He would rather let it go to foreclosure than let me get it back. My life was full of up hills battles, but this one was a major fight. After the initial phone conversation and meetings, everything went south real fast. The enemy showed up to let me know I wasn't getting anything. But I remember God saying what the enemy meant for my bad would turn out for my good and my later days would be better than my former. There were so many ugly things that occurred with us trying to get the house. My ex reneged on the agreement, we had to get an attorney to facilitate the deal, we did a quit claim deed with payment. Next it was getting my ex to leave the home after we gave the payment. After that it was a battle back and forth, police involvement, restraining orders, and court. My ex ended up leaving the premises and we moved in, but we moved into a house that had been vandalized. After moving in, we attempted to modify the mortgage because the mortgage had not been paid in over four years–since I left.

Needless to say, we received the runaround regarding the modification, several months passed without an approval. By this time, the bank started the foreclosure proceedings. Our home was up for foreclosure. I wrote the bank, called manager, went to the court to file papers, contacted attorneys and nothing. I prayed and said to God that I listened to his every word, he told/spoke to me to get the house back, therefore I couldn't understand why we were going to foreclosure. My husband and I started to look for a new home, we planned to move out before the foreclosure took place. Then God spoke again and told me to anoint the doors and windows in the home. I got some olive oil, prayed over it and anointed the doors and windows. After this there was nothing else, I could do. I remember the saying "When you've done all you could do –just stand! I held my head up high and stood still. The foreclosure was still in motion, but I had done all I could do. A few days later I received an email that the foreclosure proceeding had stopped, and the bank wanted us to fill out the modification paperwork again. I thought I was seeing things. I called the banks Attorney, not my attorney but the banks. They confirmed the foreclosure was not going to happen. My husband and I praised God all that day and night, but we knew this was only for a moment. My husband and I sprang into action. He applied for a loan to purchase the home. When we got the loan approved and called the title company to do the closing, they asked for the name of the buyer and seller and both our last names were the same. They said just like the loan officer said when my loan was approved to purchase the town house. This has never happened before. I told her that God was in the midst of this and he doesn't make promises he can't keep. I told her God had performed another miracle for me and explained how I had gotten a house right after claiming bankruptcy. We closed on that home too. This is why I do what I do and am in the insurance business. One is because I lost my Mom and Dad when I was young, and I know what it is to NOT to be able to visit my Moms gravesite. I help my clients get the appropriate life coverage for their loved ones and leave a legacy for their family. God allowed me to meet my current husband, leave my job and get my dream home back. Its' true God gave me everything back that I lost and then more. God allowed me to open my own business, the Gina S. Duncan Insurance Agency to help the people that desperately need help and to allow his will to be done in the earth through me, showing others the way, supporting those in need and being a voice for those that need me. To also make sure my family is insured and protected, for when something happens or I leave this earth one day, my children will be ok.

AFTERWORD

As you can see from these stories, you do not have to be a "Perfect Woman" or a "Super Woman;" you just have to be the "Virtuous Woman" you were created to be. Refrain from putting on titles that were created by man and not God. There is nowhere written in the 66 books of the Bible that you were called to be a "Perfect Woman" or a "Super Woman." However, Proverbs 31:10-31 outlines the pattern of a virtuous woman: who she was, how she thought, how she behaved, and what she was called to do. Who she was defined her character. What she thought defined her wisdom. How she behaved defined her courage. Last, what she was called to do defined her strength. Eliminate the pressure, weight, and the cares by taking off these pseudo-titles of "Perfect Woman" or "Super Woman," and take on what God said you are. She is a wife, mother, servant, leader, business woman, encourager, and fears the Lord. She is trusted, honored, praised, and blessed. She serves, loves, helps, and gives to others. She is skillful, cognizant, and a visionary full of faith. She invests wisely and saves her money. She is eager and excited about her work She understands and walks in her purpose.

I have heard many women say, "I do not want to be that woman." "That is too much for one woman." "I cannot be her." "I do not have what it takes to be her." My question would be, "Why wouldn't you want to be the woman God created you to be?" What is holding you back from being this woman? The challenge in this walk of being a virtuous woman who demonstrates excellence is that we get so deceived by the images we see, then we take that image and think this is what a virtuous woman is, rather than what a virtuous woman should be. "Charm is deceptive, and beauty is fleeting, but a woman who fears the Lord is to be praised" (Proverbs 31:30, NIV). Proverbs 31:30 (KJV) states, "Favor is deceitful, and beauty is vain; but a woman that feareth the Lord, she shall be praised." Therefore, the focus of your eye should not be on the perfection of the walk in becoming a virtuous woman, but rather on the progress of the walk. Each step in your walk is progression that gets you closer and closer to becoming the woman you were designed to be.

In spite of what life has brought, the failures, disappointments, and persecutions, it was all ordered to build your character, to give you wisdom, ground your courage, and stabilize your strength. If you never fail, you will never know how successful you can be. If you never follow, you will never know how great a leader you can become. If you always stay inside the box, you will never know what exists outside it. Failing, following, and stepping outside the box are actions that show evidence of your walk and your efforts. Through your walk and your efforts, God will bless you, and you will get extraordinary results. All you have to do is just start walking in the ways of a virtuous woman.

So I leave you with this final thought, Women of Virtue Walking in Excellence: "Who can find a virtuous woman? For her price is far above rubies" (Proverbs 31:10, KJV). Find that virtuous woman that is within you, and understand the value of her worth. Understand that the value of your worth is by creating value with your influence, and not your performance. In Proverbs 31:10-31, this woman's value was predicated on how she influenced everyone she came in contact with. Her husband had confidence in her and lacked nothing of value (Proverbs 31:11, NIV). Her children arose and called her blessed; her husband also, and he praised her (Proverbs 31:28, NIV). God uniquely created you to do something others cannot do. When you understand your worth, you open yourself to endless possibilities. You will never have to chase anything, anyone, or any opportunities; they will all come looking for you. You are invaluable. You are limitless! Your success, walk and the woman you are becoming are all a part of your creation! You are a Woman of Virtue who walks in excellence, with character, wisdom, courage, and strength. There is more to you than you even know. Discover and become the best version of you! Discover and become a Woman of Virtue Walking in Excellence!